LENT

The Journey from Ash Wednesday through Holy Week

Edited by Greg Goebel and Joshua Steele

Foreword by Tish Harrison Warren

ANGLICAN COMPASS

An imprint of LeaderWorks

An Anglican Compass Book
An Imprint of LeaderWorks

Lent: The Journey from Ash Wednesday through Holy Week

ISBN
Paperback 978-1-734-3079-2-4
Ebook 978-1-7343079-3-1

Text and Cover Design by Blu Design Concepts
1. Lent 2. Anglican 3. Holy Week

Published in the United States of America

Table of Contents

Foreword by Tish Harrison Warren

MY FATHER SAYS he had a high school girlfriend who gave him up for Lent. I'm not sure this is actually true. You never knew with my dad. What's evident is that most people primarily associate Lent with the practice of "giving something up." Perhaps chocolate. Perhaps my Dad.

Lent isn't exactly known for its curb appeal. Who likes to give things up? The liturgical season is often associated with the worst kind of legalism, the kind of religiosity that assumes that if you enjoy anything, then it must be really bad, or where congregants in pressed suits primly forgo coffee to score brownie points with God

But Lent, at its best, does not call us to deny the goodness of the world or its many pleasures. Nor does it ask us to work hard so we can get God to like us a bit more before Easter. Lent is a gift from the ancient church, given that we may—if we so dare—learn to be more attuned to the goodness of God, the gentleness of his love, and the astonishing abundance in this life of faith.

And this is why we need books like this one. This little book invites us into an ancient and needed means of grace. It is a book for beginners, a helpful guide to those who are curious about or new to this ancient practice. And yet, aren't we all beginners in the life of grace? The spiritual life, for all of us, often entails learning the same things, again and again and again, more deeply and clearly. In this way, this book—like the liturgical calendar itself, with its repetitive, annual cycle—will meet us all in our own context and path, whether it is our first or fiftieth Lent.

But why make a book like this now? In our cultural moment, trendy fasts and juice cleanses have become all the rage, but Christian asceticism is often derided. Much of the contemporary American church focuses on a cheerful consumerism, a faith that promises our best life now. And we are constantly told through thousands of advertisements that the good life is within our reach (or purchasing power), that it is found by "following our bliss," denying ourselves nothing that feels good or right. So why go through the pain of Lent? I suspect that in spite of numbing consumerism, there remains a deep hunger in all of us for spiritual practices that offer more than emotional experiences with a malleable God, who would never ask us to practice even the least bit of self-denial.

The call to take up a season of deprivation is not out of a pearl-clutching fear of pleasure. We do not give up chocolate or meat because they are bad but because we can be dulled through constant (often mindless) consumption so that we cannot receive these good things as a gift, but instead cling to them like an addict, to numb our pain, to dull our longing, to hush our needling sense that things are not right in the world and not right with us. We can use these pleasures to avoid reality, the reality of this world's brokenness and our sinfulness. Lent calls us deeper into reality.

Perhaps ironically, deprivation itself can make us more attuned to the enduring goodness in our lives. About a decade ago I taught English at a school in rural Uganda for a summer. Where I lived there was no running water or flushing toilets, no restaurants or television or air-conditioning. After several months, I returned to Kampala, the big city, and went to a restaurant and watched an episode of Friends (in English). On the surface, it was an unremarkable experience, but I was in bliss—never have I so relished a meal or delighted in public restrooms or found a sitcom so hilarious. Giving up the things I cling to for comfort allowed me to receive them back, not as a numbing agent or a crutch, but as a gift.

But there is an even more profound gift of Lent. Just as momentary deprivation allows us to notice the complex loveliness of the world, it also allows us to be alert to God, to enjoy God's presence, to wonder at God's passion for us. Lent is a way to lift up a tiny shot glass of suffering, not only to remember the goodness of God's gifts, but to taste the suffering of Jesus.

Ours is not a bloodless faith. Jesus did not breeze through earth, ever-victorious and cheery, to efficiently accomplish a tidy salvation. Nor did God simply send down a creed-in-a-box, to which we assent. Jesus entered into this world where he met pain, need, hunger, thirst, frustration, agony, and sorrow. He felt the weight of our sin in his very body, and, in Lent, we meditate on his suffering with and through our very bodies.

I have a friend who is a trained chef. She gives up meat and dairy every Lent. She adores butter and rich gourmet meals, so Lent is hard for her, as you'd imagine. But she isn't joylessly trudging through the season. She takes up this yearly practice with a sort of humble gusto because it teaches her to encounter God, year by year, even through her stomach.

Through these visceral physical and communal practices, we learn to worship. We learn to enjoy God, to be in awe of who God is and what God has done.

So feast on this book about fasts and rest in these words about repentance because they call us, ultimately, not simply to a season, but into the very mystery of a God who loves us, joyfully and relentlessly, and gave his very self up for us.

Introduction

"...in an abundance of counselors, there is safety" (Prov. 11:14b, NRSV)

Consider this book your abundance of Lenten counselors. Drawing from the work of 13 other contributors, we created this book to help you navigate the Church's ancient yearly journey from Ash Wednesday to Easter Sunday.

Pastors in the Anglican tradition instruct their congregations on Ash Wednesday:

> *Dear People of God: The first Christians observed with great devotion the days of our Lord's passion and resurrection, and it became the custom of the Church to prepare for them by a season of penitence and fasting. This season of Lent provided a time in which converts to the faith were prepared for Holy Baptism. It was also a time when those who, because of notorious sins, had been separated from the body of the faithful, were reconciled by penitence and forgiveness, and restored to the fellowship of the Church. In this manner, the whole Congregation was put in mind of the message of pardon and absolution set forth in the Gospel of our Savior, and of the need that all Christians continually have to renew our repentance and faith. (Book of Common Prayer 2019, 543).*

We invite you, therefore, in the name of the Church, to the observance of a Holy Lent.

In the following pages, you will learn:

- What Lent is and why it matters (Ch. 1)
- How to practice the traditional Lenten practices of self-examination, repentance, prayer, fasting, almsgiving, and reading and meditating on God's Holy Word (Ch. 2)
- How others have experienced various aspects of Lent in their own journeys (Ch. 3)

Then, in Chapter 4, we have provided "Collect Reflections" for the prayers assigned to the Sundays and Holy Days of Lent and Holy Week. In Appendix A, to guide your use of Scripture during Lent, we've provided tables of Sunday and daily lectionary readings. And, in Appendix B, we have listed some of our favorite recommended resources to learn more about the Lenten journey.

Lent is all about repentance, honesty with God, and growing into a deeper knowledge of who we are in Christ. We pray that this book helps you remember that you are dust as you prepare to celebrate that Christ has died, Christ is risen, and Christ will come again.

CHAPTER ONE

What is Lent? A Journey from Ash Wednesday to Easter

LENT IS A SEASON of fasting and penitence in preparation for Easter. It begins on Ash Wednesday and lasts for 40 days. Holy Week begins on Palm Sunday and lasts for 7 days, leading up to Easter Sunday.

Note that the entire Church year revolves around two "cycles," one for Christmas and one for Easter. Just as the Christmas cycle begins with the preparatory season of Advent, the Easter cycle begins with the preparatory season of Lent. In Advent, we prepare to celebrate the Incarnation, and we look forward to the Second Coming of Christ. In Lent, we prepare to commemorate and celebrate the Crucifixion and Resurrection.

IMPORTANT DEFINITIONS

Source: Donald K. McKim, *The Westminster Dictionary of Theological Terms*, Second Edition, Revised and Expanded (Louisville, KY: Westminster John Knox Press, 2014).

Lent: (Middle Eng. *lente*, "spring," from Old Eng. *lengten*, "to lengthen [daylight]") The period of forty weekdays prior to Easter, beginning with Ash Wednesday. It was originally a time to prepare candidates for baptism and became a period of penitence for those who have been baptized.

Ash Wednesday: The first day of Lent, forty weekdays before Easter. The practice of placing ashes on the forehead symbolizes repentance and contrition.

Holy Week: The last week in Lent, commemorating the last week of the earthly life of Jesus. It begins with Palm Sunday and ends on Holy Saturday, prior to Easter.

Palm Sunday: The Sunday prior to Easter, commemorating Jesus' entry into Jerusalem to the shouts of "Hosanna" and the waving of palms (John 12:13).

Maundy Thursday: (Lat. *mandatum*, "mandate, commandment") Holy Thursday, before Good Friday, when Jesus commanded his disciples to follow his example of service in the washing of feet (John 13:5ff.). The term derives from John 13:34, "I give you a new commandment [Lat. *mandatum novum*], that you love one another."

Good Friday: The Friday of Holy Week, before Easter Sunday, commemorated in the Christian church as the day on which Jesus Christ was crucified.

Easter (Easter Sunday): The yearly Christian festival celebrating the raising of Jesus Christ from the dead three days after his crucifixion. It is preceded by Good Friday. Easter is the first Sunday following the full moon that occurs on or after Mar. 21. The date varies between Mar. 22 and Apr. 25. Theologically it celebrates the victory of Christ over death and evil as well as Christian hope.

How long is Lent, exactly?

Lent begins on Ash Wednesday and lasts for some reckoning of 40 days—recalling Christ's fasting during his temptation in the wilderness (Matt. 4:1-11).

Traditionally, the Sundays in Lent (including Palm Sunday, for a total of 6 Sundays) are not counted toward the 40 days. Although Lent is a season of fasting, every Sunday in the Christian year is a feast day, a celebration of the resurrection of Jesus Christ. So, we do not fast on Sundays. Therefore, although there are 46 days between Ash Wednesday and Easter Sunday, the Lenten fast lasts for 40 days.

However, there have been and still are disagreements on how the 40 days are counted, whether Sundays are counted, and whether Lent includes (all, none, or a portion of) Holy Week, the week immediately before Easter Sunday. *The Oxford Dictionary of the Christian Church* [*ODCC*] overviews this history succinctly:

> "In the first three centuries the period of fasting in preparation for Easter did not, as a rule, exceed two or three days, as is evident from a statement of Irenaeus recorded by Eusebius....The first mention of a period

> of 40 days..., prob. of Lent, occurs in the Canons of Nicaea (A.D. 325; can. 5). The custom may have originated in the prescribed fast of candidates for baptism, and the number 40 was evidently suggested by the 40 days' fasts of Moses , Elijah, and esp. the Lord Himself, though till a much later date the period was reckoned differently in the different Churches."

According to the *ODCC*, the current format for Lent, where it starts on Ash Wednesday and goes until Easter Sunday, for a total of 40 days (not counting Sundays) began in Rome in the 7th century.

Why is it called "Lent"?

In Greek and Latin, the names for Lent make more sense, because they're based on the number 40. However, English is more confusing. According to the Online Etymology Dictionary (etymonline.com):

- "Lent" comes from the English noun "Lenten," meaning either "the season of spring" or the period of fasting we now refer to as Lent.

- "Lenten" comes from the Old English "lencten," meaning "the season of spring" or "Lent, the period of fasting."

- "lencten" comes from the West Germanic "langitinaz," meaning "long-days," or "lengthening of the day."

- So, "Lent" refers to the lengthening of the days during springtime.
- (Incidentally, "lentil" has a separate etymology.)

What are some common practices during Lent?

This book will give an overview of the common Lenten disciplines:

- Self-Examination
- Repentance
- Prayer
- Giving
- Fasting
- Reading Scripture

What are the main worship services during Lent and Holy Week?

Ash Wednesday

If you are new to Lent, you can go to any Anglican, Lutheran, or Roman Catholic Church on Ash Wednesday. Or find another type of church that has an "Ash Wednesday" sign.

None of the traditions listed here require that you be a member to participate in the Ash Wednesday service. Just note that Orthodox churches (Greek, Russian, etc.) have a slightly different calendar, so they often observe Lent in somewhat different ways and different times.

The service will focus on repentance, grace, and forgiveness. The readings include warnings from Isaiah about fasts that God loves. That God wants us to free the oppressed and to walk in justice. They will include Christ commanding us not to do our fasting to be seen by others.

The service will remind us that we are mortal, and that we must repent. You will be invited to come forward and to kneel. A minister will impose ashes upon your forehead, usually saying, "remember that you are dust, and to dust you shall return."

The service will be reverent and quiet. It is intended to be stark. During the service, you will be called upon to join with the whole Church in a Holy Lent. To pray that God will open our eyes to see that we can be honest with him, and repent. To see that we can tell him of our pain, and sorrow, and that he understands. He knows because Christ, God himself in the flesh, walked through his own wilderness, and then walked beyond that to the cross.

Fast on Ash Wednesday by eating only one full meal and two small portions, with no meat all day. Fasting is not for those under 14 or over 60, or anyone in poor health. If you cannot fast, give up meat or something else that day. Fasting directs our attention to our need for God and follows the example of Christ. It is an act of penitence, meaning a demonstration of heartfelt repentance.

Again, you do not have to be an Anglican to participate. If

your church does not observe Ash Wednesday, you will be welcomed in one of our Anglican churches, without having to be a member or change traditions. We're all in need of a journey of repentance together.

The Sundays in Lent

The Sundays in Lent follow a journey through the temptation of Christ, the visit of Nicodemus, the woman at the well, the healing of a blind man, and the death of Lazarus. Each of these Sunday readings guide us on a journey toward understanding the healing power of Jesus for our souls, our bodies, and our very lives.

The fourth Sunday in Lent is Laetare Sunday and its color is traditionally rose. Laetare is the Latin word for "rejoice." This may seem odd in Lent. But with Easter in sight, the idea is to help us rest in the joy and hope of the Resurrection of Christ, even in the midst of our Lenten journey. This "refreshment Sunday" is designed to remind us, once again, that the Feast is the main point. The fast is only there to help us prepare, not to condemn us or weigh us down.

Palm Sunday

On Palm Sunday, we remember Jesus' triumphal entry into Jerusalem (see Matthew 21:1-11, Mark 11:1-11, Luke 19:28-44, and John 12:12-19).

Many services on Palm Sunday begin with "the Procession of the Palms," where worshippers hold palm branches as they process into the church.

Sometimes Palm Sunday is also observed as "Passion Sunday," a commemoration of Jesus' suffering and death. However, Passion Sunday used to be celebrated on the Sunday before Palm Sunday, the fifth and last Sunday of Lent.

Holy Monday through Wednesday

Palm Sunday, Maundy Thursday, Good Friday, Holy Saturday, and Easter Sunday get the lion's share of the focus during Holy Week. However, Monday through Wednesday ought not to be forgotten! This is largely because we do not really know exactly what happened on the Monday and Tuesday of the original Holy Week.

We do know that Holy Wednesday has traditionally been called "Spy" Wednesday, as a reference to the "ambush" of Jesus by Judas Iscariot.

Each of these days can be observed however, through worship, prayer and Scripture reading.

The Triduum or "Three Days"

The Paschal (Easter) Triduum ("three days") begins on the evening of Maundy Thursday (the liturgical day beginning at sundown, just like in the Jewish calendar). The Triduum includes Maundy Thursday, Good Friday, Holy Saturday, and Easter Sunday. It ends at sundown on Easter.

Maundy Thursday

Maundy Thursday commemorates the institution of the Eucharist at the Last Supper (see Matt. 26:26-29; Mark 14:22-25; Luke 22:14-30; 1 Cor. 11:23-25) and Christ's washing of the disciples' feet (see John 13:1-15).

'Maundy' is likely derived from the Latin 'mandatum' which means basically "commandment."

Because Thursday night of Holy Week corresponds to the Last Supper, it includes Jesus saying, "A new commandment I give to you, that you love one another as I have loved you." This is the night of that New Commandment, in other words, it is New Commandment Thursday.

Maundy Thursday services traditionally include a focus on the Last Supper, not only as the beginning of the Triduum (the Great Three Days), but also as the institution of the Lord's Supper, Eucharist, Communion. In many places, a foot washing service is included, and the service often ends with the Stripping of the Altar.

Traditionally, there would be no Eucharist on Good Friday. So the altar was stripped of all eucharistic elements on Maundy Thursday. Today, the stripping and washing of the altar is often an integral part of Maundy Thursday at the end of the service.

Interestingly, this tradition developed simply because the altar guilds needed to strip the altar after Maundy Thursday in preparation for the bare, stark altar on Good Friday. People stayed after worship to observe this, and it was soon experienced as a powerful spiritual moment.

Because of this, Maundy Thursday ends with the starkness of the empty, bare altar. Our souls are bare as well, as we begin to walk through the rest of the weekend.

Good Friday

On Good Friday, we remember the events leading up to and including the crucifixion and the crucifixion itself. The Solemn Collects are read, with the leader requesting prayer for a particular purpose (like the salvation of the lost), keeping silence while the people pray, and then "collecting" their prayers in a written prayer. As mentioned above, Eucharist is not celebrated on Good Friday because this is the day in which we try to live in the reality of the brutal starkness of the cross of Christ. In some places, Eucharist is administered from reserved sacrament—consecrated bread and wine that have been set aside (for later use) during a previous service of Holy Communion.

The Gospel reading for the day is taken from the Passion narrative and is therefore quite long and is often read slowly and deliberately. The people traditionally stand when Jesus is taken to the cross, and all observe a lengthy moment of silence after Jesus dies. The readings end before the resurrection and the people depart from the church in silence.

Holy Saturday

On Holy Saturday, before the Easter Vigil, we remember the time that Christ spent in the grave. This is traditionally observed by taking time for silence and meditation upon the death of Christ.

Easter Vigil and Easter Sunday

At the Easter Vigil we gather to hold a vigil. We gathered in darkness, just as the women who went to the tomb went there before dawn.

Our vigil begins in this darkness and the light is carried into the midst of the people, and spreads. We rehearse the story of our redemption, our story. This is the story of the preparation for the Light to come into the world.

As the light grows we welcome new members into Christ's church through baptism. In the early church, this would have been the service where the catechumens were baptized and could then receive their first communion.

After the reading of the Story of Salvation, the light blazes as we celebrate the coming of the day of His resurrection, with shouts of Alleluia! And then we celebrate the first Eucharist of Easter.

It's really pretty amazing. Between covering all of salvation history in a single service, saying "Alleluia!" again for the first time since the beginning of Lent, and celebrating the Resurrection in the early hours of Easter morning, this really is a unique service! Additionally, this is the service at which people were traditionally baptized and welcomed into the Church.

On Easter Sunday, we remember and celebrate the triumphant Resurrection of Jesus Christ from the dead! Easter Sunday then kicks off a period of 50 days traditionally known as Eastertide — ending with Pentecost Sunday.

But Easter Sunday is only the beginning! A great fifty-day feast (known as "Eastertide," "Easter Season," or "Easter Time," as well as "Paschaltide," "Paschal Season," or "Paschal Time") kicks off on Easter Day. In the Church Year, this is quite literally fifty days of feasting.

Easter is the highpoint of the Church Year. So it makes sense that we would party for so long. After all, the main point of the whole gospel is to prepare us for an eternal celebration and feast.

This is reflected in the fact that our Lenten fast only lasts forty days (not including Sundays), while Easter is fifty days. Fasting will pass away, as Jesus said, but the Great Feast of the Lamb will last for ages of ages (a Hebrew into Greek idiom for eternity!).

Why fifty days of Easter Time? After the resurrection, Jesus spent forty days on earth before he ascended, and then there were ten more days after that before the Day of Pentecost.

Luke writes in the first chapter of Acts that Jesus "presented himself alive to them after his suffering by many proofs, appearing to them during forty days and speaking about the kingdom of God."

In Acts chapter two, we find the followers of Jesus gathered for the Day of Pentecost, which actually means "fifty." It happened during the Hebrew feast of Shavuot, which is why the followers of Jesus were gathering. The Hebrew festival was originally a harvest first-fruits celebration, and later it had evolved into a commemoration of the giving of the Law to Moses on Mt. Sinai.

So the Great Fifty Days are a celebration of the Resurrection of Christ and all that means for us, leading to the launching of the Christian Church and its mission on Pentecost. And our Lenten journey prepares us for that.

What's the point of Lent?

The following list is not exhaustive but consider the following Lenten lessons.

Lent reminds us that we are sinners and we need to repent.

We are sinners and we need to repent—even after we are baptized, saved, forgiven, and healed. Yes, we continue to be a part of this fallen world, and to make our contributions to it. Forgiveness from God – total forgiveness – doesn't mean that we are already perfected. He forgives us because he knows we will need it continually in this fallen world. And if you do not think believing Christians sin, then you must not be reading the news.

The model for all prayer, the Lord's Prayer, itself teaches us to pray for forgiveness every day, and the biblical epistles are full of admonitions to continually repent. So Lent is a yearly journey—as we walk the path together as a Church from Ash Wednesday to Easter— that reminds us, humbles us, and takes us back to the foot of the cross.

But it doesn't do this to condemn us. We repent to be free, to be honest with God, to be enabled to accept his forgiveness one more time. We cannot repent unless we are already assured of his love and grace.

Lent reminds us that we cannot earn God's forgiveness.

God forgives us by grace!

Lent is not about reminding God that he should forgive us, or trying to please him enough to forgive us, or to prove something to God. Instead, it's about reminding us that we worship a God who loved us enough to take away our sins, and who always will.

Every Lent we take up disciplines. We show our repentance by receiving the ashes, by our prayers, and by our desire to seek reconciliation with others. We also give things up, fast, and take up spiritual disciplines.

But we do not take on these disciplines to prove that we are righteous people. They are not a tool for healing, but for diagnosis. The medicine of the Gospel is God's grace. The Law is the diagnostic tool.

So in Lent we take up these fasts and disciplines to be better able to listen to the Holy Spirit. To see ourselves as we are. To know our own weaknesses and to observe our temptations. As we do so, we pray for God to reveal his grace to us in a deeper way.

Unless we see our symptoms and sickness, we do not seek a cure. The Lenten disciplines do not take too long to reveal something to us, and when they do we are supposed to rest in the knowledge of God's love and grace.

Every Lent, in each and every way, we fail to keep our disciplines in some major or minor way. This is a great opportunity to be reminded that failure is the point. In other words, if I finish Lent with a greater awareness of my own failings, and so am more aware of my need for God's grace and the forgiveness of others, then my Lent has been a holy one.

By the third week, or even the second week, of Lent, most of us have stopped feeling like Lent is a "cool ancient tradition." This is the time when it starts feeling like a real bummer. We want to avoid feeling gloomy, because that's not really the point of Lent, but unavoidably it happens. This too is a spiritual discipline. Walking through Lent is not about our own fortitude or about feeling "awesome" about it. It is about just doing it.

LENT

Just walking through those days on the calendar called Lent and seeing what there is to see through the experience.

The beautiful thing about time is that it marches on, despite us. We do not make Easter arrive. We do not "earn" Easter by keeping a perfect Lent. It arrives.

St. John Chrysostom preached a famous Easter sermon about this fact around 400 A.D.,

Are there any who are devout lovers of God?
Let them enjoy this beautiful bright festival!
Are there any who are grateful servants?
Let them rejoice and enter into the joy of their Lord!
Are there any weary from fasting?
Let them now receive their due!
If any have toiled from the first hour,
let them receive their reward.
If any have come after the third hour,
let them with gratitude join in the feast!
Those who arrived after the sixth hour,
let them not doubt; for they shall not be short-changed.
Those who have tarried until the ninth hour,
let them not hesitate; but let them come too.
And those who arrived only at the eleventh hour,
let them not be afraid by reason of their delay.
For the Lord is gracious and receives the last even as the first.
The Lord gives rest to those who come at the eleventh hour,
even as to those who toiled from the beginning.
To one and all the Lord gives generously.

Easter arrives regardless of how successful we are at keeping Lent. Thanks be to God!

WHAT IS LENT?

Lent reminds us that the feast is the main point.

Lent is a fast that is observed to prepare us for Easter. Because fasting, taking up disciplines, and focusing on repentance and self-denial can be very dramatic, we can make the mistake of thinking that Lent is about fasting. But the fast is not the main point, the feast is.

We were not made for fasting, we were made for feasting. God told Adam and Eve to be fruitful and multiply, to eat of anything in the garden they wanted, to enjoy his presence and each other. They were made for feasting and enjoying life. The only "no" commandment was to not eat from the tree of the knowledge of Good and Evil. Everything else was, "yes!"

But since the Great Rebellion, the Fall, we do not handle feasting well. Humanity tends to over-indulge, become addicted, feel guilty, steal our food from others, etc. Because of this, we start to think that feasting, enjoyment of life, and celebration must be bad things. We perceive that fasting is true to the spiritual life but feasting and enjoyment are contradictory to them. But nothing could be further from the truth. In fact, we fast so that we can be prepared to properly feast! Fasting is the prelude; feasting is the main event.

Jesus said this clearly when he was questioned about fasting by the disciples of John. They wanted to know why he and his disciples were not fasting. He replied, "Can the wedding guests mourn as long as the bridegroom is with them? The days will come when the bridegroom is taken away from them, and then they will fast." In other words, when he returns, we will not need to fast anymore. We'll be feasting in a great marriage supper. He says in Matthew 22 that the Kingdom of God can be compared to a wedding feast. Our fasting is preparation, it is part of this temporary phase of life. Feasting is what we are really learning to do. Feasting is our future and our life with God now. He created us to feast!

Listen to the prophet Jeremiah describing God's restoration of Israel, a foreshadowing of all of the People of God in eternity:

Then shall the young women rejoice in the dance,
and the young men and the old shall be merry.
I will turn their mourning into joy;
I will comfort them and give them gladness for sorrow.
I will feast the soul of the priests with abundance,
and my people shall be satisfied with my goodness,
declares the LORD. (Jeremiah 31:13–14, ESV)

And at the end of the Bible, when the New Heaven and Earth is described, the people are celebrating. They are enjoying God and each other and life. That's our destiny, and we will know how to really feast then. Fasting is only a temporary part of our life in this fallen world, albeit a necessary one, which is preparatory for the Great Feast.

So during Lent, we fast to prepare for Easter, a parallel to our lives of waiting for Christ's return. We do not eat cake every day of the week before our birthday. This is not because eating cake is wrong, but because we want to celebrate with enjoyment and appreciation. Cake is a special thing to be enjoyed and rightly prepared for by waiting until the proper time.

When we fast during Lent, we are not avoiding certain foods because they are inherently harmful or indulgent, but because food is sacred and special. We are preparing for the feast by reserving its special elements for the feast itself. Our fast reminds us what hunger and need feel like, so that when we feast we will know that it is God who fills us up. Part of that preparation are the Sunday feasts. The Sunday feasts in Lent are mini-Easters, celebrations of Christ's resurrection on the Lord's Day, so they are times to celebrate, to enjoy life, food, and fellowship. They are not moments of guilty indulgence, instead, they are a glimpse into the future life we are assured of in Christ. We need those weekly reminders of the future feast, even in the midst of our fast time.

Ultimately, Lent is an especially appropriate time to renew our repentance and faith as we cling to the good news that Jesus Christ—our crucified, risen, and exalted Savior—is Lord.

CHAPTER TWO

How to Observe a Holy Lent: Practices for the Journey

Why Observe a Traditional Lent?

By Greg Goebel

I'M BUSY PLANNING out my personalized Lent. I need to decide what to give up. I need to decide what to give away. I need to pick books to read and do things that are tailored to my own personal, spiritual needs.

Lent arrives soon. Am I ready? There are so many choices to make. Or are there?

A Traditional Lent

If I weren't tailoring my own personal Lenten experience, and were just following the tradition, I would:

- fast on Ash Wednesday,
- read the Bible with special attention,
- read the Church Fathers (and Mothers),
- give up sweets and alcohol (except on Sundays),
- abstain from meats on Friday (or perhaps give up one meal),
- give away extra money to help the poor,
- volunteer my time to visit and assist the sick, the prisoner, or the outcast.

The tradition is not totally uniform. But this is a basic outline of Lenten disciplines for many generations back.

Why should I craft my own personal Lent when this old, shared, practical tradition exists?

Creating a Rule of Life for Lent

A rule of life is an intentional plan of spiritual disciplines that serves as a training program to shape our attitudes and behaviors toward love of God and our neighbor.

What can be included in your rule of life? The traditional disciplines of Lent (self-examination, repentance, prayer, fasting, giving, and reading Scripture) are an excellent starting point.

If you're looking for more information or ideas for your rule of life, consider:

***The Celebration of Discipline,* by Richard Foster.** This book is a classic on the spiritual disciplines. Foster covers inward (meditation, prayer, fasting, and study), outward (simplicity, solitude, submission, and service), and corporate (confession, worship, guidance, and celebration) disciplines.

***Soul Feast,* by Marjorie J. Thompson.** Thompson

lists spiritual reading, prayer, common worship, sabbath and rest time, fasting, self-examination and confession, spiritual direction, and hospitality.

***Emotionally Healthy Spirituality*, by Peter Scazzero.** Scazzero lists Scripture, silence and solitude, Daily Office reading, study, sabbath, simplicity, play and recreation, service and mission, care for the physical body, emotional health, family, and community.

***The Common Rule*, by Justin Whitmel Earley.** Earley covers daily (kneeling prayer three times a day, one meal with others, one hour with phone off, Scripture before phone) and weekly (one hour of conversation with a friend, curate media to four hours, fast from something for twenty-four hours, Sabbath) habits for a modern rule of life.

What I'm Not Saying

I don't want to imply that we are doing something wrong when we make personal decisions about our practices during Lent. Not at all.

This is all about repentance, honesty with God, and growing into a deeper knowledge of who we are in Christ. It isn't about following rules or rigidly maintaining a tradition for its own sake. In fact, even within this tradition, choices have to be made about where to give money and where to serve.

But we can be so very quick to assume that we are totally unique individuals that should always be making personal choices for ourselves, curating a plan of action from our options. And that can become a problem when we start to see ourselves as above the tradition, rather than within it.

Try a Traditional, Not Tailored, Lent This Year

So this year, consider not personalizing your Lenten experience. Consider simply doing what has long been done.

Consider just being one of the many Christians around the world who are giving up meat on Fridays or abstaining from sweets. Consider reading the Daily Office and picking up an ancient Christian reader. *(Just note also that, traditionally, there are exceptions on fasting for young children, pregnant women, anyone who is ill, and the elderly.)*

Don't tailor it. Don't select from it. Don't fret about it. Just do it. Perhaps it will be freeing to not make many choices this year, walking through Lent the way an older generation did, and seeing what happens.

Of course, no matter what we do, we can't really do it. We'll fail in some way. Even if we totally succeed and we nail it, we will still probably suffer from pride in ourselves for the accomplishment. And that is the point of Lent. The point is not to do it just right, but to walk through it with each other, in the grace of Christ.

Maybe this year is the year to ***not*** do your own thing for Lent?

Preparing for Lent *By Lee Nelson*

Prepare for Lent by renewing a sense of its true purpose: making room for new life to spring up.

The great Paschal Feast of Easter is always celebrated in the Western Church on the first Sunday after the first full moon following the spring equinox, when the days are neither long nor short.

Why this connection to the moon and the sun, to seasons and daylight?

Ancient Christians understood themselves to live in the cosmos, inside of God's good creation. They understood that Christ's salvation did not only extend to the human soul, but to the whole of creation. Celtic Christians, for instance, include animals, the sun, the moon, and trees in their carvings and manuscripts because of this innate understanding. To be clear, this is not an expression of pantheism, the idea that all of creation shares in the nature of God or the gods, but the understanding that all of creation is created by God, to be redeemed by God, and that all of it serves as a signpost to us not only of his goodness, but of the very doctrines of the Christian Faith.

New life springs forth from dead seeds, and limbs stripped

of their leaves bring forth new leaves every spring. To see this is to be catechized in a Gospel which, as opposed to rejecting creation, speaks of its being reconciled. As Paul writes, that in Jesus "all the fullness of God was pleased to dwell, and through him to reconcile to himself all things, whether on earth or in heaven, making peace by the blood of his cross." (Colossians 1:19–20 ESV)

So it needs to be said that Lent is about dying. But it also needs to be said that Lent is about asking God to bring about new life in us. We are a people who have died with the Lord Jesus Christ in the waters of Baptism and have been raised with him to newness of life. This is not a one-time occurrence. Rather, it is a process which, beginning there, continues through one's life. When we fast, it is about desires and impulses dying in us to make room for new life. When we give something up, it is to make room for something else—something better, something good, something life-giving.

The purpose of the Lenten disciplines, then, is to make room for new life and actually take up that which is life-giving. This, above everything else, takes prayer. Without prayer, spiritual-discipline is emptied of its true purpose—that of drawing you up into the life of God.

We can prepare for Lent by focusing on that true purpose, and it is then that we are ready for self-examination in the context of grace and life.

Self-Examination *By Erin Faith Moniz*

Self-examination is the process of asking God to show us the truth about ourselves so we can be healed. Some tools for self-examination are confession and reconciliation, using a rule of life, and meeting with a spiritual director, counselor, or trusted friend to review your spiritual life in the past year. Self-examination is best done with the support of a trusted, graceful guide.

Frederick Buechner, in a reflection on Lent, makes this observation: "Jesus went off alone into the wilderness where he spent forty days asking himself the question what it meant to be Jesus. During Lent, Christians are supposed to ask one way or another what it means to be themselves." (*Listening to Your Life: Daily Meditations with Frederick Buechner)* This kind of self-examination is common and valuable for the season of Lent. We turn to disciplines of meditation, confession, and repentance. We fast so as to strip away the distractions that might keep us from learning about the deep parts of ourselves where the Spirit needs to transform us. Lent is a spiritual curation process where we submit ourselves to a time of reflection and surrender.

However, this process is shrouded in fear and misunderstanding, prompting many to be suspicious of Lent and its purposes. Some are afraid to participate in self-examination because they are wary of intense legalism that they have experienced in the past. Many are both drawn to and fearful of self-examination. Anything with the word "exam" in it gives most of us heart palpitations, and the practice of self-examination in conjunction with repentance conjures up puritanical images of self-flagellation and soul-crushing penitence. In a culture where the worst kind of sin we can commit is the sin of having low self-esteem, our frantic veneer of positivity leaves no room for a season like Lent. Who would want to willingly open themselves to the frightening possibilities of self-examination and submission when a myriad of soft-lit distractions abound?

But let's redirect any suspicions you might harbor about Lent and self-examination. First, Lent calls us to both personal and corporate disciplines. Many of us are used to the self-help culture of personal reflection where we privately muse on our own life only to become judge and jury of our destiny. Meditation or practices like the Ignatian (or Wesleyan) Examen are helpful during Lent and allow for valuable self-reflection. But if we only depend on these private reflections, we are still vulnerable to the possibility of vapid conclusions. Lent calls us to meditation and confession.

Ignatius of Loyola's Daily Examen

The following practice of prayer, usually done at the end of the day, was made popular by Ignatius of Loyola's *Spiritual Exercises*, where it is referred to as the "General Examen."

Here is how Ignatius described the Examen:

- "The first Point is to give thanks to God our Lord for the benefits received.

- The second, to ask grace to know our sins and cast them out.

- The third, to ask account of our soul from the hour that we rose up to the present Examen, hour by hour, or period by period: and first as to thoughts, and then as to words, and then as to acts, in the same order as was mentioned in the Particular Examen.

- The fourth, to ask pardon of God our Lord for the faults.

- The fifth, to purpose amendment with His grace."

If confession makes you just as nervous as self-examination, remember that it can be a helpful counterbalance to meditation. If first we reflect on ourselves and God's work in us, we can then take these observations to a safe, discerning communion of believers. You may not have grown up with this discipline, but confession is a beautiful fruit of the Church that allows us to journey together by unburdening our hearts and experiencing hope and forgiveness from those who know and love us (Gal. 6:2). Confession, when executed in the tradition of the church with care, absolution, and love, is a remarkable way to bring light into the darkness of our lives. In *Seeds of Hope*, Henri Nouwen writes, "Often someone's careful and honest articulation of the ambiguities, uncertainties, and painful conditions of life gives us new hope. The paradox is indeed that new life is born out of the pains of the old." Resulting from self-examination, we need to share our confessions and hear the confessions of others. This is an essential premise for the next reason we practice self-examination: freedom.

A powerful tool of the enemy is convincing us to ignore or hide our sins and flaws. There is a popular and effective lie that our brokenness is much worse when revealed and it would be best to keep it in the darkness of secrecy. Yet, Scripture says that because of Christ, we are free (Gal. 5:1). We are children of the light who are not bound by condemnation (Rom. 8:1; Eph. 5:8; 1 Thess. 5:5). Self-examination is a frightening enterprise when we associate it with a burden of slavery. But reflection and confession are not tools of slavery, but avenues of freedom. They break the lies that keep us captive and draw us back to our identity in Christ where we know ourselves again as sons and daughters of God lacking nothing for life and godliness (2 Peter 1:3). If self-examination is not leading us to a corporate experience of freedom, then we have missed the point.

This practice is neither privatized nor self-effacing. Instead, asking God to show us ourselves in a defined season is an essential exercise in the freedom of our salvation. It is, in essence, a continual flourishing of our salvation. It is the means of our *metanoia* ("repentance") both within and with the corporate body of believers. Fredrick Buechner asserts that the road of meditation and confession can be painful.

"It can be a pretty depressing business all in all, but if sackcloth and ashes are at the start of it, something like Easter may be at the end."

We learn a lot from nature. Often, the parables of Jesus use the order and rhythms of creation to teach spiritual truths. During Lent, we start in the thick of winter. Ash Wednesday comes in the midst of a hard, cold winter where we can look as far ahead of us as we can behind and see the long silence of this wintery season. Winter appears on the surface to be a season of death and stagnation, but nature knows better. The detritus of Autumn has left the marks of life teeming just below the surface. In the dark, the seeds find their bearings and begin to absorb the nutrition around them. They wait, but their waiting is not passive. More goes on than we perceive from the surface. The first echoes of Spring are whispering below our feet. What looks like death is not death at all, but life.

In *Living the Sabbath: Discovering the Rhythms of Rest and Delight*, Norman Wirzba writes, "To be a servant of creation is to seek to live according to its rhythms and in sympathetic alignment with its potential but also its limits." During Lent, our spiritual rhythms run parallel to nature's rhythms. We embrace the silence and self-examination of the season with the knowledge that our waiting is not the same as inactivity. Like nature, we wait without being spiritually passive. We submit to a process because we believe, like winter's seeds huddled beneath the frozen topsoil, that God is growing us and filling us. We believe, like the prayer attributed to St. Francis of Assisi, that it is in dying that we are born again to eternal life. Nature teaches us how life comes from death, and we focus ourselves on this lesson during Lent. We let our layers be stripped away because we, along with nature, are being prepared for Spring and new life.

Repentance *By Greg Goebel*

When we have prepared our hearts with a reminder of God's grace and allowed the Holy Spirit to guide our self-examination, we can pray that God will turn our hearts to repentance. Repentance can take on many forms. In some cases, it is helpful to make amends to anyone we have harmed, if possible. In any case, we put into practice an amendment of life.

We wretched and miserable sinners.

Some will be offended, as these words seem rude and unworthy of creatures created in God's image. To retain these words would be to wrongly imply that human beings are supposed to grovel before God and debase themselves.

Others will be pleased, as these traditional words seem to capture the full spirit of repentance and our total need for God. To abandon them, they say, would be to trust too much in ourselves.

Which approach is correct?

As in many things, the words themselves matter. And when

these words were chosen from the English lexicon in the 17th century, they meant something slightly different than they mean today. And that may be the key to understanding what our Lenten liturgies mean. I will not digress too long into word study but hang with me for two sentences.

Miserable and wretched today are often associated with words like "detestable" or "odious."

Yet in the 17th century, they were more likely to be understood as meaning "helpless" or "poor" or "without aid."

There is a bit of a difference there. When our liturgies tell us we are "wretched" sinners, they are reminding us that we need God's intervention. We need to be saved. We cannot save ourselves; we are helpless without Christ.

So "you wretched sinner" means "you poor person who cannot save yourself." To repent, then, is to admit that I cannot save myself. That I need Christ. That I need help.

We aren't odious or detestable to God. He loves us. He made us. But we do need his help, and without it we cannot be saved. He loves us enough to show us that pretending otherwise doesn't help. Repent (tell the truth).

But are we "sinners"?

Yes, we are. We are all sinners.

The problem with the word 'sinners' today is more of a 20th-century problem. In the 20th century, many people were taught that there are the good people, and then there are the sinners. The good people are the ones who get saved, and then keep trying to be holy. They attend church. They raise a family. They do not cuss or swear and they keep a steady job. These people are good people. Even today, you'll hear people say, "He is a good Christian man." Sometimes this is a way of saying, "He's not a sinner like some other people I know."

The sinners are the ones who do not attend church much, swear a lot, and drink, smoke, and chew.

To be clear, this way of thinking of sin is terrible. It has nothing to do with the Bible or with the Christian faith, and it has hurt millions of people's faiths.

If this is what you've been taught, Lent can be a terrible time. You may be thinking of all those religious, good people and wishing you were one of them. Maybe this Lent I'll finally break through and be as holy as that other person, and not such a sinner. Your Lent might be spent debasing yourself and groveling or trying to find the right discipline that will make God smile upon you.

Or worse, you may be thinking that you are pretty good, and that Lent isn't such a big deal for you as it would be if you were one of the truly bad sinners. Your Lent might be spent counting the days in which you didn't sin and rejoicing that there seemed to be only two or three "little" sins.

Well, sinning is a lot deeper than that. It is a disease at the core of every human that affects everything we do, and that no one is immune from.

And sin is not just the bad things that an individual does or does not do. It is also the broken and unjust ways that we organize our nations and societies, to the benefit of some over others. Repentance in Lent includes acknowledging our part in injustice, as the Prophet Isaiah wrote,

> Is such the fast that I choose,
> a day for a person to humble himself?
> Is it to bow down his head like a reed,
> and to spread sackcloth and ashes under him?
> Will you call this a fast,
> and a day acceptable to the LORD?
> "Is not this the fast that I choose:
> to loose the bonds of wickedness,
> to undo the straps of the yoke,
> to let the oppressed go free,
> and to break every yoke?
> Is it not to share your bread with the hungry
> and bring the homeless poor into your house;
> when you see the naked, to cover him,
> and not to hide yourself from your own flesh?
> Then shall your light break forth like the dawn,
> and your healing shall spring up speedily;
> your righteousness shall go before you;
> the glory of the LORD shall be your rear guard.
> (Isa. 58:5–8, ESV)

To repent, we must open our eyes to any injustice we

participate in and demonstrate penitence by becoming involved in freeing others from oppression.

Deeper Issues of Repentance

Repentance involves both our individual and corporate sin, but it also involves what is called sins of omission.

There is something in the Anglican service that really makes me uncomfortable. It is not something I encountered often before I experienced the classic Christian liturgy. At the Confession of Sin, we pray: "Most merciful God, we confess that we have sinned against you in thought, word, and deed, by what we have done…" and the next phrase rattles the bones, "...and by what we have left *undone*."

What I have left undone? I remember the first time I prayed this confession; I wasn't sure I wanted to pray that part. Even things left undone? Where is the wiggle room in that?

We are honest, us churchgoing folks; we work hard to stay away from the sins of commission. These are the things we actively do to harm ourselves or others. We really focus on those. Do not lie, Do not cheat, Do not steal, Do not commit adultery. It is not that we succeed in putting those sins away; it is just that we learn either to hide them, or we work hard to stay away from them. They are the object usually, when sin is the subject.

Holiness, our churchy version of it, is learning to avoid the really obvious things we do to harm others. Holiness, in our minds, is more about the "Do nots" than it is about the "do's."

What we religious insiders do not want to face is the reality that our fallen nature goes deeper than just what we do. We are also sinners because we leave undone the things we ought to do. We are not just to avoid harming others, to stay in our houses, to mind our own business.

Unfortunately, according to Jesus, it is a sin to "mind my own business." At least, if minding my own business means ignoring the pains and sorrows of others.

Jesus was the one who said, "Do unto others as you would have them do unto you." He didn't merely say do not do anything harmful (that too). But he goes beyond that to give us the positive command to actively treat others with love. To serve others. To heal others. To carry the burdens of others.

If we aren't doing that, we are missing the mark, and we have sinned against God, others, and ourselves. And that is what makes me uncomfortable. I'm pretty sure I deeply believe that I'm doing pretty good as long as I do not harm anyone. I do not want to face the reality that I'm sinning just by ignoring another person's suffering. Lent is our chance to be honest about what we have left undone, and to repent.

This can all be very uncomfortable. But discomfort is a good thing for us. We need to see the truth, the truth that we need salvation and healing from the inside out.

In all of this, remember that Jesus is not condemning us, ever. Jesus is giving us a doctor's diagnosis. He is the Great Physician, not the Great Fitness Trainer. He is showing us that we need to be healed from the inside out. He is the one healing us.

And so the Confession of Sin during Lent reminds us that holiness is love. To be holy as God is holy is to actively love others. Love is never passive, it is active. And it reminds me that since I fail to actively love others, I am failing to be holy. That realization is the moment of crisis. Will I hide away from God because I've seen my own sin?

Thankfully, we get to hear these words after our confession of sin and repentance:

> Almighty God have mercy on you, forgive you all your sins through our Lord Jesus Christ, strengthen you in all goodness, and by the power of the Holy Spirit keep you in eternal life. Amen.

Repentance is about radical honesty in the face of a holy God, but a holy God who has issued absolution and removed condemnation. It is about no longer hiding away from him, as if he doesn't already know my heart. It's about speaking the truth out loud.

Lent helps me face the truth. It calls me to a deeper level of honesty, while also covering me in the absolute grace of Almighty God, through the Incarnate Son, in the Spirit's power. I do not love others actively as I should, and I'm forgiven for that, and then strengthened in all goodness, kept by the power of the Holy Spirit.

So we're all sinners, and that's actually good news. Because it means that we're all in this together. There aren't "good people" and "sinners." There are just people. We are a "fallen race," not a few fallen people. This is good news because it means that God hasn't asked us to try to work harder to become one of the good people. He himself is actually saving us and healing us. We need this; we cannot heal ourselves (we're wretched, remember?).

So this Lent, embrace your wretchedness through acts of repentance. Be honest about your misery. Own up to your sinfulness. Prepare the way of the Lord, make straight paths in your heart. This is the day of salvation.

Prayer *By Lee Nelson*

We pray during Lent by following the Lord's Prayer, learning as we go, and by not seeing ourselves as masters of prayer, but as those who want to experience God. During Lent, consider taking up a special time of daily prayer.

Jesus said,

> When you pray, do not heap up empty phrases as the Gentiles do, for they think that they will be heard for their many words. Do not be like them, for your Father knows what you need before you ask him. Pray then like this: "Our Father in heaven, hallowed be your

> name. Your kingdom come, your will be done, on earth as it is in heaven. Give us this day our daily bread, and forgive us our debts, as we also have forgiven our debtors. And lead us not into temptation but deliver us from evil." (Matthew 6:7–13 ESV)

The words of Our Lord from the Sermon on the Mount set forth those very words that have formed the backbone of Christian prayer since the very beginning, a way of praying, not with many words, but with the simplicity of children, honoring their Heavenly Father, asking for their daily needs, praying for their forgiveness, and invoking protection against all evil. The Lord's Prayer, it has been said, sets forth the pattern and practice of prayer.

It is a pattern very much like the sort of pattern one would use in sewing a dress or a shirt. I remember when I was a child, my mother enjoyed sewing from patterns. She would lay out the fabric, pinning the pattern to the fabric, and carefully cutting out each piece. Patterns are necessary because, without them, the product of our labors is rather haphazard and disjointed. We need a pattern of prayer because intentionality and order in prayer are precisely the things that lead us to fruitful prayer. The Lord's Prayer is like a trellis for a vine—without a trellis, the vine will be untrained and unfruitful. What we find in the Christian life is that, as opposed to shaping prayer to our own lives, it is we who are molded to prayer.

The Lord's Prayer sets forth the practice of prayer in that, in regularly reciting it, our own prayers flow out of the simplicity and the goodness of the Lord's own prayer to the Father—not empty phrases, or many words, but the prayer of one who is already known by God.

All of this is to say that, if you are struggling with prayer, perhaps it is time to give up on seeing prayer as something you do and start seeing it as a gift of a loving Father, who invites you to speak, in simplicity and trust, of those desires of the heart he already knows. Teresa of Avila once remarked, "Prayer is loving intercourse with God." She said this because she knew the intimacy of knowing God, not so much as a friend, but as a marital lover. Perhaps that scandalizes you, but it is precisely the heart of Christian prayer—all at once a sacredness, intimacy, and even a hidden, private love which brings joy to the heart and trust to our wills.

In Lent, prayer comes into focus as a discipline, meaning that it requires the heart of a learner. Consider taking fifteen minutes a day to come to the Lord and ask him, as did his disciples, to teach you to pray. Slowly, and with the intention to learn, take up the Lord's Prayer. Let the words wash over you. If distractions come, simply tell them to wait until the fifteen minutes are over. When you are finished, take the time to truly listen, and in the end, give thanks for that time.

If you struggle to keep up the discipline, remember that you are learning. Most of us are, in truth, still learning to pray. Ask the Lord to help you. Ask for the grace to be attentive and to be given the gift of prayer. What you will find is that the practice of prayer is what gives shape to discipline, and not only discipline, but great joy and growth.

Fasting *By Lee Nelson*

Fasting is, in part, giving up some or all food for a period of time. But we can also fast from other things such as eating out, using a mobile device, or eating desserts. Please keep in mind that young children, the elderly, and anyone with a health condition that precludes fasting should not fast from all food but may want to choose an alternative. Some choose to fast from particular foods, or to eat only very basic, bland foods.

If you are new to fasting, you may want to choose to fast from one meal on Ash Wednesday and Good Friday, and to give something up (for example, alcohol or sweets) during Lent, except on Sundays.

One of the forgotten things about sin is that it not only introduces disruption between human beings and God, but disruption and alienation in our innermost selves. We experience this, as did Saint Paul, as a war within our members, a battle between flesh and spirit. The objects of our desires are not typically evil; they are also part of God's good creation. What we find is that it is the desire itself that is disordered. Saint Augustine called this "concupiscence," a desire for any good in general, but more specifically the desire to feed our lower and sensual appetites. This refers not only to the appetite for food, but for sex, power, money, and even more innocuous things like control over our schedules, time to ourselves, and having things in their place. These are not bad things, not at all, but again, our disordered appetites are the problem.

What are we to do? The body must be trained to yield up its most basic desires. If we are to gain the interior change and sanctification that God is working in us by His grace—seeking to bring order where there is disorder—then fasting is in order, and Jesus assumes that his disciples will do it. But they are not to do so publicly, lest it merely feed an appetite for the good opinion of others. So, he says: "When you fast, do not look gloomy like the hypocrites, for they disfigure their faces that their fasting may be seen by others. Truly, I say to you, they have received their reward. But when you fast, anoint your head and wash your face, that your fasting may not be seen by others but by your Father who is in secret. And your Father who sees in secret will reward you." (Matthew 6:16–18 ESV)

One can fast from anything that assaults the appetites. The purpose of fasting is to bring about hunger in order to put those appetites in their proper place. So, food is not the only possibility. One could fast from eating out and the experience of endless choices. One could fast from speaking of others in a judgmental or derisive way. One could fast from yearning for power or advancement.

But, nearly always, fasting from food is the most basic kind of fasting. Here are a few recommendations:

First, start with fasting from a specific type of food that you crave. This could be sweets, meat, coffee, fatty foods, alcohol, salty foods, etc. These types of fasts need to last about 40 days to be effective, so Lent is a good time to start. Regular breaks on set intervals are to be expected. This keeps us from pride. This is the reason that during Lent, the Church considers fasts to be canceled on Sundays, as they are feasts of the Resurrection. Many people regularly fast from meat on Friday, as an example.

Second, move to fasting from solid food, starting with a daytime fast that lasts until an evening meal, and then moving to 24-hour fasts that go from dinner one day through dinner the next, going up to 36 or 40-hour fasts. These should always include the consumption of fruit juices to keep up energy and blood sugar. These fasts are the norm for Ash Wednesday and Good Friday.

Third, if you can do the second without suffering much, consider longer fasts, up to 5–6 days, or repeated days in which no meal is taken during daylight.

What I think you'll find is that your appetite for the things of the self is put in check and that you'll notice the subduing of the body and its desires. This aids in the flourishing of an active spiritual life.

Giving *By Lee Nelson*

Lent is a time for giving. We give something up in Lent to help us learn about ourselves, and our relationship with God. We give something away to serve our relationship with our fellow people.

Almsgiving is not a word that we use often today. We will often speak of "mission support" or "charity" or something akin to "philanthropy." These terms certainly speak of the mission of God, or of His call to us to be a people of love, but the traditional term for the Lenten discipline has been simply "almsgiving."

Almsgiving is not only charity given to those in need, but a merciful kind of giving, characterized by pity. Pity does not usually have a positive connotation today, but it is essentially the proper human response to the sight of wretchedness—that of tenderness, compassion, and care. We might say that almsgiving comes by being moved to compassion when we see the plight of others, not in a remote sense, but in a direct sense. Almsgiving, then, concerns our neighbors, especially those who bring us distress.

Mother Theresa used to speak of the poor as "Christ in his distressing disguise." Jesus himself makes reference to this when he says: "I was naked and you clothed me, I was sick and you visited me, I was in prison and you came to me." (Matthew 25:36 RSV) To lend compassion to the naked, the sick, and the imprisoned is to love and have mercy upon our distressing neighbor in an incarnate way, in the flesh.

Almsgiving expresses interior conversion with regard to our neighbor, while fasting expresses interior conversion with regard to ourselves, and prayer expresses interior conversion with regard to God. What we find is that the Holy Spirit is at work in us to truly sanctify our selfishness when it comes to the plight of our neighbors. Jesus holds up before us the image of the Good Samaritan, who stops to come to the aid of his neighbor, beaten and bloodied on the road. He not only pays for a room, but he personally takes care of the details. This required looking a distressing image of humanity square in the face and acting in total selflessness.

I would challenge you, this coming Lent, to pray that the Lord would show you his face in the most distressing of your neighbors and lead you to ways that you can show compassion and mercy.

There was a man who used to sleep on the grounds of my former parish. He was definitely insane, given to fits of rage and erratic behavior. He would defecate on our wheelchair ramps and spread trash all over the place, which of course my staff and I had to pick up, nearly every day. When we decided to offer small kindnesses to him, a bottle of water, a half of a sandwich, a pair of new shoes, not only did his demeanor change, but he became something of an honorary security guard, personally keeping watch over the parish. He cleaned up after himself. He even let a local charity give him a haircut. Through this man, wretched and distressing as he was, I learned just how much the Lord intends the kindness of his people to be a light in this world. You never know what almsgiving might do for those you serve, and for your own soul.

The prophet Isaiah focused on this aspect of the fast, prophesying that the fast is "to share your bread with the hungry and bring the homeless poor into your house; when you see the naked, to cover him, and not to hide yourself from your own flesh." (Isaiah 58:7, ESV) The fast of Lent is a time for compassion, not self-righteousness.

Reading Scripture *By Greg Goebel*

Despite its focus on repentance, Lent is no exception to the gracious focus of all Scripture—Jesus Christ himself. Scripture is always about redemption.

How should we read Scripture in Lent? Before we look at that question, we have to lift a few burdens. First, not all of us are expert Bible scholars, and that's okay. As the Church Father Tertullian said, "Your faith has saved you, not your skill in the Scriptures." Second, the Bible's main purpose is actually not to be a collection of moral tales that help us cope with life, although it does provide that. Third, the Bible that we use has numbered chapters and verses so that we can find specific places. However, it is not intended to be broken down into minute, numbered lines that overwhelm us. Having lifted those burdens, we can be free to engage with the Bible in the way the Holy Spirit inspired it.

The story of the Road to Emmaus in Luke 24 is one place to start. Here Jesus goes through all of the Old Testament, Moses, and the Prophets to show how they reveal him. That's right, the Old Testament's purpose is to reveal Jesus Christ!

John 3:16 is really the key to all of Scripture: "For God so loved the world that he gave his only Son, that whoever believes in him should not perish, but have eternal life."

We will not always understand all of the details of Scripture, and there are many confusing places. But the main point of the Bible is to prepare the world for the coming of Christ, to reveal that coming, and to call all men to salvation in him.

For an example of how the Bible works, consider the story of Joseph in the book of Genesis. Joseph can be read as a moral tale of patience, trust, and humility. And it is useful to see it that way, but to only see it that way misses the main point. To get a handle on the big picture, let's review Joseph's story. He is loved by his father but misunderstood and resented by his brothers. He is put in the ground, left for dead. He is falsely accused and put again in the ground in jail. Then, by a miracle, he is raised up to the King's right hand. He uses his position of power not to destroy his brothers, but to save them. In fact, he saves his own Hebrew family, along with the Egyptians, by storing up and distributing grain to everyone. He places his family in a safe place in Egypt, along with the Egyptians.

Sound familiar? Jesus is loved by the Father, but his own people and all people misunderstand him. He comes to the earth but is misunderstood, resented, and finally crucified and buried. By a miracle of God he is raised up and seated at God's right hand. But instead of using his power to destroy us, he uses it to save us. Jew and Gentile, together living in reunion with God and each other. He provides for us from the storehouses of his grace.

The Holy Spirit inspired Scripture, so these historical stories are true, though they are related to us through the People of God and the language and culture of their day. Not all the details directly relate in every way. And yet they are given to us to prophetically reveal God's love for us through the incarnate Son.

The Bible is our family history—the good, the bad, and the ugly. It's all there, and Scripture doesn't hide from the truth. But also there is God's intervention in our history, bringing about reconciliation from alienation. The individual stories of each human being (ours too!) intersect with the family history of the human race, and all flow back to Jesus Christ.

Lent is no exception to the gracious key to Scripture. Paul wrote that there is now no condemnation in Christ Jesus. Jesus came to save us, not to condemn us. Lent, though focused on repentance, is a time of grace, no less than any other time. And reading Scripture in Lent is a continued reading of the story of grace.

We bear fruit when we experience these stories in light of the big story, allowing the love of God to be told to us again and again. We are transformed when the Holy Spirit opens our ears to truly hear and believe that God does indeed love, forgive, and heal us. And when we listen to the stories of those around us, and tell them the story of God's love, they are called from estrangement from God's family back to restoration and peace through Christ.

Using a Lectionary to Read Scripture in Lent *By Winfield Bevins*

A lectionary is simply a list of Bible passages for personal reading and study, or for preaching in services of worship. Later in this guide (Appendix A, p. 142), we have included Scripture lessons (readings) from two common Lectionaries for reading in Lent.

Prayer and Bible study are inseparably linked. Scripture should always be read in the context of prayer, because prayer is the medium that brings us into contact with the same Holy Spirit who inspired the authors of the Bible. As we read the Scriptures, the Spirit applies the truths of the Word to our hearts. Prayer is the necessary means whereby we understand the Word of God. Without the assistance of the Holy Spirit in prayer, our Bible study will be in vain.

Our tradition of Anglicanism arose out of the Reformation, and from its inception proclaimed that the "Holy Scriptures containeth all things necessary to salvation." Strongly influenced by Reformation thinkers of his day, Thomas Cranmer wholeheartedly believed in the importance of spending time in the Scriptures daily. This explains why the Word of God functions as the very foundation of the Book of Common Prayer, which is saturated with Scriptures from the Old and New Testament. Cranmer once said, "The people (by daily hearing of holy Scripture read in the church) should continually profit more and more in the knowledge of God and be the more inflamed with the love of his true religion."

For Cranmer, Scripture and prayer hold to one another through an intricate connection. In his mind, these pillars of the faith should not be separated. Cranmer's vision for the Daily Office was a matrix of prayer and Scripture woven together, exposing the reader to the presence of the Living Word. Cranmer's collect for the second Sunday of Advent shows his intimate love for the Scriptures:

> Blessed Lord, who hast caused all holy Scriptures to be written for our learning; Grant that we may in such wise hear them, read, mark, learn, and inwardly digest them, that by patience, and comfort of thy holy Word, we may embrace and ever hold fast the blessed hope of everlasting life, which thou hast given us in our Saviour Jesus Christ. Amen.

Thomas Cranmer's vision for Anglicanism included reading Scripture daily throughout the year. He restored the ancient practice of reading through the entire Bible in daily prayer. His greatest desire was to put the Bible and prayer in the hands of ordinary people so that they would be in a place where the God of the Bible could transform their hearts and lives. This is why Cranmer devised a Bible reading plan (lectionary) through which everyone could hear the Scriptures on a regular basis.

Reading the Bible, however, can be a little overwhelming at first because of its sheer size and the extent of its different doctrines, characters, stories, and themes. But there is good news: we do not have to be systematic theologians to read and understand God's Word. Reading the Bible is more like a marathon than a sprint, so I recommend that you start small and finish big. It will take a lifetime to study the entire Bible, and even then, we will never know all there is to know about it.

Lectionary tradition is a historic and systematic way that every Christian can read and hear the Scriptures throughout the Christian year. The Book of Common Prayer contains this systematic Bible reading plan. The lectionary readings from the Book of Common Prayer are used for daily services of worship and for Morning and Evening Prayer. In Cranmer's first Prayer Book of 1549, the lectionary appeared as a guide for twelve months, January to December, and provided Old Testament and New Testament lessons for every day of the year. Cranmer intended the Scriptures to be read at Morning and Evening Prayer so that they would become ingrained into the daily rhythms of peoples' lives.

Since that time, there have been many versions of the daily lectionary. Some lectionaries go through the Bible in a year, while others follow a two- or three-year cycle. Many of the most recent lectionaries are designed for Sunday services of worship and adhere to the church calendar. In recent years, there has been a move toward uniformity among the various lectionaries, such as the Revised Common Lectionary. Regardless of which lectionary or Bible-reading plan you follow, there is nothing more important than a regular reading of the Scriptures.

Cranmer poetically said, "In the Scriptures be the fat pastures of the soul." This means that the Scriptures are the very place where we encounter the Lord and where he feeds us with his daily bread. It was Cranmer's deep hope that, in this way, all Anglicans would hear, read, mark, learn, and inwardly digest the Scriptures. Just as Moses encountered God in the burning bush, we also come face-to-face with God through the Scriptures. A. W. Tozer reminded us: "The Bible is not an end in itself, but a means to bring men to an intimate and satisfying knowledge of God, that they may enter into Him, that they may delight in His Presence, may taste and know the inner sweetness of the very God Himself in the core and center of their hearts."

CHAPTER THREE

Personal Reflections from the Lenten Journey

A Long Obedience in a Lenten Direction

By Jack King

Re-learning the Lenten Basics

A week before Ash Wednesday, I was preaching at a Christian high school to students who are just learning about the season of Lent. I find excitement sharing the basics of spiritual seasons like Lent to people who are learning about the Christian calendar for the first time. As I teach others, I find myself learning the basics all over again. I discover new insights in my own life with God while I teach the basics of the liturgical year.

Take the basic framework of the Lenten season—forty days, not including Sundays, that remembers Jesus' temptation in the wilderness. The basic theology here is that Jesus redeems Israel's story and her failure to trust the faithfulness of God during her sojourn from Egypt to Canaan. Where Israel rebels, Jesus obeys. When Israel pines for Egyptian slavery again, Jesus abides in the Father. When Israel molds and worships a golden calf, Jesus refuses to bend the knee to Satan. At every stage of Jesus' wilderness testing, he proves himself faithful to the

Father. This is the essential story that frames the whole season of Lent.

I described that basic Lenten framework and added the notion that the Jesus story is meant to shape my own story. Because I'm called to grow in the likeness of Christ, I'm also called to practice obedience with my whole self—body, mind, and soul. The forty days of Lent are given to awaken me to that calling.

And yet I'm naive and foolish if I think that I'll be able to perfectly obey the Father for forty days as Jesus did in the wilderness. Forget forty days—I'm not capable of living one day of total repentance and perfect obedience. I desire the perfect obedience of Jesus in my life, but I'm not capable of achieving that measure of faithfulness in my own strength.

A Lifetime of Lents

As I shared this basic framework for Lent, I saw a new dimension of the Lenten experience. I need a lifetime of Lenten seasons to learn full obedience to Jesus. There can be an implicit pressure at the beginning of Lent to "get everything in your spiritual house in order." Ash Wednesday is a great wake-up call for the places where I've been negligent in my life with God. But Lent is not a spiritual crash diet. It's impossible to get everything in order in my heart over one Lenten season. I do not need one Lenten season. I need decades of Lenten seasons to train me in Christlikeness. Lent trains me in a humility and patience that the Way of the Cross is a lifetime journey, not a temporary trek for 40 days.

Because my calling to Jesus lasts a lifetime, I need to think about growth in repentance over many years, not just one Lenten season. As Eugene Peterson said, we are called to practice "a long obedience in the same direction." As I practice repentance—the turning of my whole self to God—it's obvious I will need a lifetime of Lenten seasons to mature into the likeness of Christ.

I would love to take on a more rigorous fast, to devote myself to prayer in a more pure and intensive way. But I do not mature in body, mind, and soul all at once. I grow by degrees. Change happens slowly. As Søren Kierkegaard said, "One should be able to tell the age of a tree from its bark; in truth one can also tell a man's age by the intensity of his repentance."

But the intensity of faithful repentance grows over years, not days. It's taken me several years to adjust my expectations for this pace of growth. My projections for growth usually outstrip my own capacity for endurance. In the past, I've not been honest with my limitations and my lack of spiritual strength. It's like trying to resume weight training after a decade away from the gym. Do not try to bench press 250 lbs. on the first lift without a spotter, or you are likely to crack your sternum. Better to work with lighter weights and build strength more slowly rather than being sidelined from discouragement or injury.

While Lent trains me in an acute attention to repentance, it also trains me in a long obedience of turning my whole self to God. Practicing the spiritual disciplines of prayer, repentance, and fasting during Lent trains us for faithful obedience the rest of the year. Lent is a catalyst for faithfulness along the Way of the Cross the whole year round. To repent, fast, and pray for only 40 days out of 365 isn't very substantial. In fact, if we never practice self-denial the other 325 days of the year, our faith will become fragmented from the rest of our lives. Forty days isn't sufficient to free us from self-absorption.

And yet, even if I commit myself to repentance beyond Lent, practicing self-denial will not be an achievement of my own penitent works, lest anyone boast. Unless the grace and strength of the Holy Spirit accompany my spiritual disciplines, all my spiritual labor would be in vain. Practicing spiritual disciplines is my response of obedience; spiritual growth is the work of the Holy Spirit, not my own.

Practicing Lent in Community

And here is one of the best graces the Spirit gives in this long obedience: the Church. I do not practice repentance in isolation. Practicing a long obedience in a Lenten direction happens in community. I will not arrive at the end of this journey by myself. When I assume new disciplines in my own strength, I have underwhelming-to-moderate growth. When I practice new disciplines in community with others, we grow much more together.

And isn't this Paul's vision of the Church? No single individual matures into Christ, the Head of the Body, by himself. The Church's calling is to

> [build] up the body of Christ, until we all attain to the unity of the faith and of the knowledge of the Son of God, to mature manhood, to the measure of the stature of the fullness of Christ...we are to grow up in every way into him who is the head, into Christ. (Ephesians 4:12–15, ESV)

As we complete this Lenten season, remember the Lenten journey lasts many years. But also remember where the Lenten journey ends. At the end of our journey we behold the resurrected Christ, the firstborn of the dead, who transfigures many sons and daughters into the fullness of his resurrection life.

How I Avoid the Deadly Sin of Gluttony in Lent *By Gerald R. McDermott*

Last week when I was in Egypt, a young earnest Anglican asked me how Anglicans fast. I was giving nine lectures on Anglicanism to sixty Egyptian Anglican bishops, priests, deacons, and their wives at a Coptic retreat center outside of Cairo. Bishop Mouneer Anis, bishop of Egypt and leader of the Global South, was my host.

I told this young man and the audience that Anglicans have fasted in different ways in their long history, but that a common standard was threefold:

- no food before Sunday morning Eucharist,
- no food on Fridays before 5 PM, and
- going without alcohol, meat, and desserts during Lent.

The audience laughed and laughed.

"Why are you laughing?" I asked. No one wanted to answer. After my talk was finished, I approached an Egyptian priest and asked him to tell me the reason for the laughter. "They laughed because your tradition seems so easy. Most Christians here do not drink at all. Meat is very expensive and so rare. And desserts are a luxury."

This priest's response has reverberated in my head over and over ever since, as I walk the Lenten pilgrimage trying to join Jesus in his forty days of fasting to prepare for his public ministry. Especially when I think about gluttony, one of the seven deadly sins. My new Anglican friends in Egypt have given me more reason to take this sin seriously.

Gluttony in the Bible

I've been somewhat surprised to discover that gluttony is all over the Bible.

It's right at the beginning, involved in the Fall. Eve took the forbidden fruit because, among other reasons, it was "good for food." As the later tradition concluded, this was an instance of gluttony because it was the quintessential example of what gluttony is—an irrational consumption of food. Irrational in this case, and to the utmost degree, because God had threatened death to anyone who ate it.

The Book of Proverbs suggests that gluttony leads to deception, disgrace, and poverty.

> "When you sit to dine with a ruler...put a knife to your throat if you are given to gluttony. Do not crave his delicacies, for that food is deceptive." (23:1–3, NIV)

> "A companion of gluttons disgraces his father." (28:7, NIV)

> "Be not among drunkards or among gluttonous eaters of meat, for the drunkard and the glutton will come to poverty, and slumber will clothe them with rags." (23:20–21, ESV)

For the prophet Ezekiel, gluttony is connected to a lack of concern for the poor. The sin of Sodom was that the residents of that cursed city were "overfed and unconcerned—they did not help the poor and needy" (16:49, NIV).

In the Gospels, Jesus was accused of being a drunkard and a glutton (Matt. 11:19). His apostle Paul treats gluttony as a kind of idolatry and worldly-mindedness. He talks about "enemies of the cross of Christ...[whose] god is their stomach, and their glory is in their shame. Their mind is set on earthly things" (Phil. 3:19, NIV).

In his second letter to Timothy, Paul does not mention gluttony by name but identifies what the medievals would later identify as gluttony's chief characteristic: love of pleasure. Paul implies the danger that this love will substitute for love for God. "In the last days...people will be...lovers of pleasure rather than lovers of God" (2 Tim. 3:1–4, NIV).

What is gluttony?

As was so characteristic of him, Thomas Aquinas subjected gluttony (which both pictures and legend suggest was a temptation for him) to precise analysis. He said gluttony is an inordinate desire for food. Inordinate because it is contrary to reason. So when a man eats more than what the body reasonably needs, and when he does so simply to satisfy the desires of his palate, he risks gluttony. (All of what follows is from Summa Theologica 2.2 Q148.)

Thomas said there are three kinds of gluttony.

1. The first kind lusts for food that is prepared "too nicely or daintily," which seems to mean refusing to eat anything other than the most carefully prepared delicacy. The Caroline divine Jeremy Taylor provides us with two examples of this: the sons

of Israel who got sick of manna and demanded flesh, and the sons of Eli who were not satisfied with boiled meat and demanded roasted meat (Holy Living chap. 2, sect. 2).

2. The second kind of gluttony is eating too much.

3. The third is when we gobble our food down in a rush or with greed, failing to take the time to appreciate it and fellowship with others.

Why is gluttony bad?

Thomas said that gluttony is a deadly sin if someone is willing to disobey God's commandments in order to obtain these pleasures. But if he eats too much or greedily yet would never do so if he knew he was breaking God's law, it is only a venial sin.

Thomas added that the sins of the flesh are less serious than the sins of the spirit. Adam was guilty of both pride and gluttony at the Fall, but it was his pride, not his gluttony, that got him expelled from the Garden.

But Thomas detailed all the dangers that come with gluttony. At this point he added immoderate drinking to immoderate eating, as the Bible often does. First, gluttony and drunkenness dull the understanding. He cites Ecclesiastes 2:3 (in the Latin Vulgate: "I thought in my heart to withdraw my flesh from wine, that I might turn my mind in wisdom") to say that fasting increases wisdom. Second, they lead to unseemly joy, where everything is always a joke and nothing is serious.

Third, they lead to excessive talking, and fourth, to immoderate behavior because they loosen one's inhibitions. Finally, he says, they lead to uncleanness of body (nocturnal emissions and vomiting).

If even half of this is true, what does it say about the explosion of food fetishes all around us? By that I mean the obsessive way that some of us have of insisting on eating only gourmet food, refusing to eat anything but "clean" food or organic food, or living with the overarching goal of always finding the positively best way of cooking the most exquisite ingredients. In other words, what should we say about being a foodie? Can we be foodies without being gluttons?

Here's a shot at answering the question. Jesus often went to parties and banquets, told parables about banquets, invited his apostles to a last supper before he died, and said that the new earth would be dominated by a wedding feast. Yet he also said the Kingdom of God is not about food and drink (Rom. 14:17).

Augustine seems to sum up the proper balance: food is not the problem, but how we seek it and why can be problems. We should eat for nourishment and also for community and friendship. The best eating is when we combine the two. Eating for pleasure alone can make us a slave of food. Keeping this balance in mind can help us avoid the deadly sin of gluttony. That is food for thought for me during Lent.

Unnatural Cravings *By Rachel Wilhelm*

Learning to Love Lent

The very first time I gave anything up for Lent, I did it with a desperate heart: not sure what I needed, not sure what I wanted, and not sure what the whole thing was about anyway. I was raising and homeschooling three growing children, teaching literature at my homeschool co-op, running 30+ miles a week, and leading music at my local Anglican parish part-time. I wanted to do this Lent thing right. I was fairly new to the Anglican faith, and thought I knew about spiritual things. I became an expert at denying myself with food, personal time, and excessive exercise. Besides, I loved the whole idea of Lent. Musically it is where I land well with minor keys, visions of cellos, repentance, and endless wilderness. Every song I write is an attempt to make someone cry.

A Minty Obsession

Believing that I knew myself incredibly well, little did I know that I was running my body down to the nubs, wearing myself out in ways that I had no idea. One of the few things that I could not control was this pesky Life Saver's Wint-O-Green mint obsession that I had. I know that sounds harmless, but it wasn't. I am not even sure how it got started. One day I craved them, bought them at the store, and that was the end of it. I kept buying bags and bags to the point that I would buy them in bulk at Costco and go through several in a week. At some point, it was all I ate. I started to get picky too; I would open up a mint, and if the mint did not have the right crunch and burn and was instead soft, I would throw it away and move on to the next. I got so used to this weird way of thinking that I did it without thinking at all, and soon I would wake up in the morning with pains in my salivary glands, craving the mints before I got out of bed. I didn't feel like myself, but I thought I knew myself.

This Lent, I was going to give the mints up. I was strong, good at self-denial, and I could shake this mint habit better than anyone could. But the thought of giving them up seized up a desperate feeling, like the thought itself was even more than I could bear. I needed those mints. I woke up every morning with a horrible tug at the base of my tongue and a jolt in my stomach. It was beyond craving. Before Ash Wednesday, I hurriedly ate up my stash in preparation for denial. The first day was hard. All I could think about was eating a whole bag of mints. The satisfaction of crunching on them and feeling a burn was so strong a temptation that I was almost wild with cravings. I tried to eat substitutes. And I lasted for days, but finally I broke down and bought a bag of mints and ate the entire thing. I couldn't believe I had failed. It was like the instinct in my body had taken over, and I had no self-will, or control. And did I mention that through all this I was tired? I was still forcing myself to run most days, and while I was teaching my children, I would take little naps between math problems, and they would have to shake me awake to check their answers. I thought maybe I had narcolepsy, but whatever, I'd beat that too.

PERSONAL REFLECTIONS

When I failed my Lenten fast, I finally did some introspection. I found that no matter how much I prayed to replace the mints; I could not shake the horrific cravings I had. I found that my body was stronger than my will, and even my spirit, and I had no room to listen for a single moment. Until I failed. My brain actually thought my cravings were normal up until I failed. My body unnaturally tricked me into believing that I needed Life Saver's Wint-O-Green mints like I needed water, or food, or maybe a drug. And then I started to wonder if maybe something was wrong with my body. So like any rational human being, my next step was to Google it. I took a day researching an obsession with Wint-O-Green mints. I looked through articles, chats, columns, and forums.

And then I found it. There was someone else out there, believe it or not, that had the same thing happen to them. Their story was the same exact story of mine, except they realized it was an unnatural craving much sooner and figured out the problem: I was anemic and was having pica symptoms. Because of iron deficiency, I was craving the crunch and burn of unnatural things, ravenous and unsatisfied. The person claimed that after a month of iron supplements, the cravings went away completely. The thought sounded impossible to me, but I immediately started to take iron supplements and she was right. Almost a month later, I did not crave a single mint. And I haven't craved them since.

Learning to Acknowledge Our Frailty

What I learned through this was that even though I believed that I was an expert at self-denial, God had other ways to show me that my human frailty can overpower my pride and self-will. I believed I was strong in my body and mind, and yet, I could not stop myself from eating a simple Life Saver. God's grace was allowing me to fail so I could see where the root of the problem was to bring it healing. What was irrational became rational: I started eating actual food, I stopped sleeping so much, the cravings for a crunch and burn simply stopped altogether. And isn't this what God wants of us during Lent? To be righted, to see clearly our frailty and come to Him with all of it, allowing the Spirit to restore where we are broken and diseased, to hear from Jesus himself and to know that the same strong cravings we have in our self-denial are the ones our souls have for the Bread of Life himself?

This was a very hard lesson for me and I never want it repeated again. But in this I was shown what is natural, unnatural, and even supernatural. The goal in our wilderness is to imitate the One who walked the wilderness perfectly, knowing his own frailty not by denying his humanity, but taking it on and trusting his Father. In the knowledge of my body's broken state, I could find the tools to heal its unnaturalness and know what supernatural things to ask my Father for. It is not in self-denial that we find who we are in Jesus; it is in knowing our frailty that we know just how much Jesus himself conquered.

A Millennial Lent *By Cameron Robinson*

I belong to the generation that no one appears to understand: *The Millennials.* We have been referred to by the "e" word (entitled), and some spend thousands to purchase books and attend conferences in an attempt to understand this "everyone gets a trophy" generation. It's pretty wild.

We are the generation that grew up with the rise and transformation of the information age. We went from Saturday morning cartoons in our youth, to 9/11 in elementary school, all the way to the invention of Siri, Alexa, Samantha (not real), and H.G. (not Wells, but "Hey Google..."). Apple's iPhone grew up with us.

Although information was at our fingertips, tradition seeped away. Some of our parents passed on a devotion to the Church, while others deemed it something that only their Grandma made them go to on Easter and Christmas.

This is where it gets interesting. For millennials, most things in our life have a point. Each app serves a different purpose and caters to my preferences. I'm writing this reflection on Google Docs because I can either sit at a desk or write on my phone.

My technology caters to me. But my faith doesn't.

My faith is personal, yet above me.

The Christian faith is individual, yet transcendent. My faith requires something of me; it reorients me from a world that *seems* to serve me, to a world that *actually* serves me. So many people have been told "just come to church" because you are supposed to. They are offered no true reason for the faith or why they should belong to their Grandmother's parish. Rather, they are told to just come because it's what you're supposed to do and no member of the family has not been "saved."

Many in my millennial generation call bluff. Why? Because so many of them are already living through hell. They are already living a life that they are deeply aware isn't satisfying. They have tried all the old tricks: drugs, technology, sex, career. Only to never discover that "Whoever wants to be my disciple must deny themselves and take up their cross and follow me. For whoever wants to save their life will lose it, but whoever loses their life for me will find it" (Matthew 16:24–25, NIV).

My fellow millennials may not use the word "disciple", but I believe they want the life and peace that discipleship with Jesus provides.

The gospel is the opposite of what we fallen humans think is normal. To lose ourselves to fasting and prayer, to Christian community, to the needs of our neighbor is the process and the map to actually finding ourselves, for our true identity is in God. In Lent, God calls us to peace.

Lent should not be tradition for the sake of tradition.

We might pass along traditions with good intentions, but

people long for community, long for something bigger, someone stronger than the present world, an answer to the issues of social lacking, a way out of what feels like hopelessness, a pulpit that points them to the sacrificial nature of the cross. A way that is both costly and fulfilling. My generation needs this hope and truth.

My generation willingly volunteers for CrossFit and Keto diets, submitting ourselves to physical sacrifice, yet remains aware that these commitments are also lacking something. I believe that deep below the distractions of our modern age exists a longing that must be satisfied by the creator. We are longing for someone not to judge us, but to welcome us into a different life, a life of sacrifice.

Lent could be the Christian church's recruiting season.

Lent should be the time where we invite ourselves and our neighbors to the sacrificial life of faith.

This is the time to invite. It's counterintuitive, but imagine the difference in discipleship when we say, "If you have that gnawing feeling inside that, no matter what you try or do, it's not enough, then I want to invite you to something else—the life of the Cross."

We model the life of the Cross after the life of Jesus, who, as the Prayer Book puts it, "*went not up to joy but first he suffered pain and entered not into glory before he was crucified.*" We already know what it feels like to suffer in a sense. We already know what it feels like to embrace the pain of a "connected society" only to be so lonely. So let's invite our lonely neighbors to a time of reflection and reorientation.

What if we spoke to our neighbors in the following way?

"As you choose to deny yourself something this Lent, I want to walk with you as you begin to receive something. This something is going to be so grand. It's going to start on the inside and feel like light pouring in. It's going to make you smile and help you begin to realize that, as St. Francis put it, 'It is in giving that we receive, it's in pardoning that we are pardoned, and it is in dying that we are born to Eternal Life.' I want to walk with you as you find this out for yourself, as this 'religious language' begins to make sense. I want to walk with you so that you are not alone, but also so that you realize that you've never been alone and will never be again. If you'd allow me to share my struggles and joys with you during this time, I'd be honored. I'm so excited for what God has for you, and I'm excited for you to lose what you've been longing to be free of."

This Lent, I pray that the gospel would free you to reach that friend or family member that frustrates you. I pray that the gospel would free you to be loved yourself. I pray that the gospel would set all generations free to eternal life.

Do We Really Need "Good" Friday?

By Greg Goebel

Should it not be called "Bad" Friday?

It was a horrible thing that we human beings killed our own creator. He came to us in lowly form, as a poor baby in a manger. He taught, he healed, he preached, he loved, he forgave. And not in spite of his grace and love, but because of it, we could not bear him. He so radically challenged our fallen human system that we had to get rid of him. He had to be sacrificed.

And yet he offered himself up as a sacrifice. No one could force Jesus to go the cross. He gave himself up…for us. In order to prove to us that we do not need to appease him with our sacrifices, our God, the Christian God, came to live among us. He gave himself as the ultimate sacrifice. It is finished. How much stronger can God say to us that we do not need to sacrifice ourselves and our children to appease him? He came here and let us sacrifice himself! Nothing is left for us to sacrifice on earth. We've even sacrificed God.

Do we really need a sacrifice?

Why would God enter our world, be a human, and then allow us to kill him? It really sounds barbaric to many ears today. It sounds barbaric because our Christian faith itself teaches us that we should not kill. It teaches us that we do not need to sacrifice our children, as our pagan ancestors did. It teaches us that God does not demand appeasement. "I do not desire sacrifice or delight in the blood of bulls and goats."

So why the need to walk through the crucifixion on Good Friday? Why do we revisit the sacrifice of Jesus every Sunday during communion? Why not excise all this talk of blood and sacrifice?

During the Reformation in England, the reformers were tempted to do just that. They noticed that people believed that the priest was re-sacrificing Jesus on their behalf in every Eucharist. They worried that people would forget that the ultimate sacrifice had already been made. And yet when they looked at Scripture, they saw the language of sacrifice everywhere, including the New Testament. What to do? Cranmer solved this conundrum when he noticed that the Old Testament included two types of sacrifice. One was the once-a-year sacrifice on the day of atonement, for the sins of the people. The other was a "sacrifice of praise and thanksgiving." He added the phrase "of praise and thanksgiving" after "sacrifice" to the liturgy to retain the sacrificial language, and also to remind us that we are not re-sacrificing Christ. We are, instead, offering a sacrifice of thanksgiving as we participate once again in his once-for-all sacrifice. We receive his body and blood just as in OT times the priests would consume the food from the sacrifices.

But this all still leaves us wondering why it is so important to talk about the cross on Good Friday and every Sunday. Aren't we past all this sacrifice stuff? Who is tempted to sacrifice their children, or an animal, or some other bloody sacrifice nowadays?

The "god" vs. the gospel

Actually, we are all deeply tempted every day to sacrifice ourselves, our children, our everything to appease the "god." The "god" is our false conception of God. It is a deep part of our fallen human nature. Every human being deeply senses that he must appease the god. Sacrificing to appease the god is as old as human history. It is who we are. It is what we do.

In today's world, we may have turned away from the "bloody sacrifices" of our ancestors (although some would say our modern warfare indicates we haven't). Our addictions prove we still offer our bodies up to the god. But even when we do not kill our physical bodies, we offer our souls, our children, our careers, our sexuality—anything—to stop the sounds of shame, guilt, and fear, or to satisfy the ruthless demands of pride. Anything to stop it! Appease the god!

Even as Christians who know the Gospel, and who believe in God's unmerited grace, we are tempted to sacrifice ourselves to earn his favor or trust. Go to church on Sunday, live a holy life, stop being a grouch, etc. All good things, but they are so easily turned into sacrifices to appease the god. Human cultures have sacrificed everything we are, everything we have. St Paul says that ultimately we believe we are sacrificing to God, but in reality, we are sacrificing to the demonic. God does not require our sacrifices.

So on Good Friday, we once again represent Christ crucified. The Gospel of Christ crucified calls to the deepest need of all humans to rest in God, to know that he has done it, and we look to him and are saved.

Day Thirty-Nine *By Erin Faith Moniz*

Forty days of Lent. This timeframe which we carve out every year before Easter hearkens back to Jesus' forty days in the wilderness at the beginning of his public ministry. But there are many forty-day stories. During their forty years in the wilderness, the Israelites ate manna for forty days until they came to a habitable land (Ex. 16:35). Moses was on the mountain for forty days (Ex. 24:18). The rains stopped after forty days during the great flood (Gen. 7:12). In all of these stories, the fortieth day is the day when there is finally a reprieve. The angels arrive with food, the rain stops, the anxiety of the past thirty-nine days is relieved.

When I was in college, God and I were finally having honest conversations.

Unfortunately, those conversations usually revolved around my unpredictable angst. I remember one indelible conversation where I found myself at the end of my patience. I told God that all these unanswered questions were ridiculous. I didn't have to take this. I thought our relationship was better than this silent treatment I was getting. I held my faith out the proverbial window and threatened to drop it if God did not come through. "I'll do it," I warned him. And I will never forget something that came to me in the quiet of my mind. I remembered the forty days.

"Remember," he prodded, "the fortieth day is the day when all questions are answered and every striving is reprieved."

"Yes," I conceded.

"Well, do you think you could live with this decision if you knew you were giving up on day thirty-nine?"

It struck me. I knew I could not live with the idea that, with everything God and I had been through, I would just give up when day forty was on the horizon.

Finding God's goodness in the wilderness

Lent is forty days. It is a wilderness time of self-examination, repentance, confession, fasting, and hope. The family of the global church enters this season together with eyes wide open. We know that while these forty days can be hard, they are good. They are good not just because they will end on Easter morning, but because they are good in and of themselves.

My college self did not wake up the next day and have the heavenly food of angels feed my questions. I did not see day forty for a while, but I knew it was coming. The divine intervention on that day was enough to keep me groping through the dark. In her book *Learning to Walk in the Dark*, Barbara Brown Taylor reminds us that it is not spiritually healthy to always aim for comfort and light. Despite the fear of wilderness seasons where darkness evokes difficulty, she confesses: "I have learned things in the dark that I could never have learned in the light, things that have saved my life over and over again."

My day thirty-nine lesson was not to pacify me until the finish line. Hope is not about shutting our eyes until the rain stops. That hope reminded me that staying in the dark season was worth it because we learn invaluable lessons in the wilderness. The traditional disciplines and themes of Lent are all long-held traditions we revisit during this time in the church calendar. Seasons like Lent and Advent call us back to the wild, uncharted places where we submit ourselves to the powerful work of the Holy Spirit in us and around us. Taylor writes,

> We are never more in danger of stumbling than when we think we know where we are going. When we can no longer see the path we are on, when we can no longer read the maps we have brought with us or sense anything in the dark that might tell us where we are, then and only then are we vulnerable to God's protection.

Let's become infants again and enter the wilderness with Christ, depending not on our own strength but returning to the sovereignty of our Lord. These forty days become a pattern of life, because the wilderness does not necessarily follow the church calendar. Our seasons of darkness come at us sideways and when they do, our legs become jelly. Our souls quiver like my college-aged self, crying out for closeness. The forty days of Lent are an echo to all our other forty-day wildernesses where we cannot tell if we are on day thirteen or day thirty-nine. But even after day one hundred and five, day forty brings the angels and the merciful blessings of the darkness are illuminated by the dawn. Lent is our invitation and as we go, we submit to a process that sharpens us for the unexpected darkness we encounter throughout our lives. We are broken open and filled afresh because, whether in Lent or Eastertide, we are never alone.

CHAPTER FOUR

Lenten Collect Reflections: Signposts for the Journey

IN THE ANGLICAN TRADITION, a "collect" (pronounced KAH-lekt) is a specific kind of written prayer. According to the ACNA Catechism,

> *Collects capture a specific spiritual theme, sum it up, and bring it before the face of God, asking for his attention and response. The word "collect" comes from the task and action of the officiant/ celebrant in collecting all the prayers of the faithful at an event in which the specific theme is in focus. Collects are at once deeply theological yet simple in construction. They are designed to be poetic and memorable, so as to captivate both head and heart, turning them toward God (To Be A Christian: An Anglican Catechism, p. 115).*

The following "Collect Reflections" are written reflections on the collects from Ash Wednesday through Easter Sunday.

Ash Wednesday *By Peter Smith*

Almighty and everlasting God, you hate nothing you have made, and you forgive the sins of all who are penitent: Create and make in us new and contrite hearts, that we, worthily lamenting our sins and acknowledging our wretchedness, may obtain of you, the God of all mercy, perfect remission and forgiveness; through Jesus Christ our Lord, who lives and reigns with you and the Holy Spirit, one God, for ever and ever. Amen.

Dusting Is the Worst

There are many household duties that I do not mind, and even some that I somewhat enjoy. Vacuuming is one of those. Then there are those chores which I cannot stand: the true *chores*. For my wife, vacuuming is one of those (we make a good couple). But I cannot think of anything worse than **dusting**.

I remember dusting the house when I was a young boy. I recall the frustrating work of unloading the shelves of books and frames, wiping each shelf, and then loading everything back on. Of finding a chair to stand on to reach the fan blades. Of wiping down the windowsills. Of removing the residue from the dining room table and giving it a rub-down of lemon oil.

I think the reason I do not like dusting is that it seems to stir up something which was otherwise stagnant. Dust is just there. It's not bothering anybody. It's not unsanitary. It's just minding its own business. You really do not notice it until you look closely or when the light hits it just right.

Dust Is the Worst

But we seem to recognize innately that dust should not be there. It's something to be removed, even if we're not interested in doing the removal ourselves. Yet, when we are tasked with the work of dusting, no matter how good a job we do, inevitably dust is kicked up into the air and then settles again on the same shelves, blades, sills, and tables which we just cleaned. (Maybe this is why it is called "dusting" and not "un-dusting.")

My distaste for dusting hasn't improved since moving to Phoenix, Arizona. Here dust is more ubiquitous than ever. This is the Wild West. Dirt is dust. It's outside floating in the air, settling in thin layers on everything around with seldom any rain to wash it away. It makes its way inside, adding to the coating of dead skin and organic matter which rests on furniture and decorations.

Now, I like living in Arizona. But dust is a bigger part of my life than it's ever been. We have weather events here—called haboobs—in which the main players are dust and wind. Air quality is a challenge and many people deal with respiratory problems as a result. Dust here is more dangerous, more violent than in the East. Dust could very easily be considered something worthy of disdain.

Yet, God Loves Dust

Yet, as the collect for Ash Wednesday says, God hates nothing he has made—dust included. Whether it's the dust in the empty lot next-door, the dust saturating the air, or the dust in living rooms, God does not despise this created matter. Neither does God despise you and me.

From the very beginning you and I have always been dust:

> *"...then the Lord God formed the man of dust from the ground and breathed into his nostrils the breath of life, and the man became a living creature" (Gen. 2:7, ESV).*

Our dust-stuff is always there, though it's been divinely fashioned into something more approachable: the stuff of bone, muscle, sinew, organ, and skin.

However, humans frequently take more drastic measures in disguising our dust: clothes, cologne, jewelry, make-up, you name it. All of this means that we often fail to see our dust-stuff. Though our bodies are presently on trajectories of decay which promise a swift return to the dust from which we came, we've found ways to forget. We've even found ways to disguise and excuse our countless offenses against God—Sin—through which we purchased and punched the tickets for our cursed, grave-bound journey.

Remember, You Are Dust

But, as it is with everyday dust, when we look closely or when the right Light hits us, then we can see ourselves for what we truly are.

We can see that apart from God's forming words and His Spirit's breath we lack existence and substance. We can see that apart from divine deliverance our corruptness of spirit has led to the corruption of our bodies. The season of Lent, which we begin with this collect, calls us to remember that we are dust, just like Ps. 103:14 (ESV) says that God always "remembers that we are dust."

Dusting, God's Way

But while Lent begins with Ash Wednesday, it doesn't end there.

When God created human beings in his image, God took something inanimate—dust—and gave it animation. He took something lowly and made it lofty. He took something dirty and made it clean.

This is no different in God's re-creation of human beings, as the collect prays: "Create and make in us new and contrite hearts." Lent ends when the spiritual dust of Ash Wednesday is transformed from inanimate to animate, from lowly to lofty, from dirty to clean.

The First Sunday in Lent *By Joshua Steele*

Almighty God, whose blessed Son was led by the Spirit to be tempted by Satan: Come quickly to help us who are assaulted by many temptations, and, as you know the weaknesses of each of us, let each one find you mighty to save; through Jesus Christ your Son our Lord, who lives and reigns with you and the Holy Spirit, one God, now and for ever. Amen.

We Serve a God Who Is Merciful and Mighty to Save

"Almighty God, whose blessed Son was led by the Spirit to be tempted by Satan"

Because Lent lasts for forty days, not counting the six Sundays which are celebrations of the Resurrection, it recalls Christ's fasting during his temptation in the wilderness (Matt. 4:1–11; Mark 1:12–13; Luke 4:1–13).

On the first Sunday in Lent, the three-year Sunday Lectionary cycles through Matthew's (Year A), Mark's (Year B), and Luke's (Year C) accounts of Jesus' wilderness temptation. As opposed to Matthew and Luke, who give us much more detail about the temptation of Jesus in the wilderness, Mark's account is extremely brief. Here's the entire Gospel lesson in Year B:

> *In those days Jesus came from Nazareth of Galilee and was baptized by John in the Jordan. And just as he was coming up out of the water, he saw the heavens torn apart and the Spirit descending like a dove on him. And a voice came from heaven, "You are my Son, the Beloved; with you I am well pleased."*

> *And the Spirit immediately drove him out into the wilderness. He was in the wilderness forty days, tempted by Satan; and he was with the wild beasts; and the angels waited on him. (Mark 1:9–13, NRSV)*

Matthew and Luke give us the specific content of the temptations Jesus faced from Satan in the wilderness:

1. "If you are the Son of God, command these stones to become loaves of bread." (Matt. 4:3, NRSV; cf. Luke 4:3)

2. "If you are the Son of God, throw yourself down; for it is written, 'He will command his angels concerning you,' and 'On their hands they will bear you up, so that you will not dash your foot against a stone.'" (Matt. 4:6, NRSV; cf. Luke 4:9–11 [Luke puts this as the third temptation])

3. "All these [kingdoms] I will give you, if you will fall down and worship me." (Matt. 4:8–9, NRSV; cf. Luke 4:5–7 [Luke puts this as the second temptation])

But still, even in Mark's brief account, we can catch the stunning point:

We serve a God who knows what it is like to be tempted and tried. We serve a God who has been in the wilderness.

This ought to be an encouragement to us, because we are tempted and tried! We often find ourselves, as it were, in the wilderness. This is where the collect goes next.

"Come quickly to help us who are assaulted by many temptations,"

But wait. When was the last time you were tempted to:

- command a stone to become bread?
- cast yourself down from the pinnacle of the temple?
- fall down and worship Satan in exchange for the kingdoms of the world?

I do not know about you, but I frequently find myself tempted to do things like:

- put my own needs above everyone else's
- mistreat others
- lie
- lust
- give full vent to my anger

Does Jesus really know what we're going through if he faced such unique temptations?

Yes, he does. Even though his temptations had to do with his unique role as the Son of God, these "edge cases" demonstrate that, if Jesus has faced these 3 "ultimate" temptations, as it were, he can relate to those "lesser" temptations we face every day. Because we serve a God who became incarnate—who became fully human for the sake of our redemption—we serve a God who knows what we're going through.

But that's not all.

"and, as you know the weaknesses of each of us, let each one find you mighty to save"

See, we do not just serve a God who can both sympathize and empathize with us in our weaknesses. Sure, sympathy and empathy are great. But they are of little comfort if the following isn't also true:

We serve a God who is mighty to save!

God both (1) **knows** what we're going through and (2) **is able** to help us. He is merciful AND mighty. I'm reminded of Psalm 103:13–14 (NRSV), which reads:

> *As a father has compassion for his children, so the Lord has compassion for those who fear him. For he knows how we were made; he remembers that we are dust.*

God is merciful. Thanks be to God! However, just before that, verses 11 and 12 read:

> *For as the heavens are high above the earth, so great is his steadfast love toward those who fear him; as far as the east is from the west, so far he removes our transgressions from us.*

God is merciful AND mighty. He knows what we're going through, and he is able to do something about it!

He is not content to let us remain captive to Sin and Death.

No, he will not let Sin and Death have the final word over his good creation! Instead, he is mighty to save. He can, today, set us free from sin's power. And, one day, he will set us free from sin's presence.

So, when you and I face temptations this week, we can take heart, for we serve a God who is both merciful and mighty to save us from our sins.

The Second Sunday in Lent

By Lincoln Anderson

Almighty God, you know that we have no power in ourselves to help ourselves: Keep us both outwardly in our bodies and inwardly in our souls, that we may be defended from all adversities that may happen to the body, and from all evil thoughts that may assault and hurt the soul; through Jesus Christ our Lord, who lives and reigns with you and the Holy Spirit, one God, for ever and ever. Amen.

Admitting Our Powerlessness

One of the great false teachings of the modern age is the supreme power of will supposedly possessed by humans. This is especially true in the modern West, where such value is placed on individual freedoms—whether economic, social, or sexual—that the notion of the sovereignty of God is typically placed as secondary to the sovereignty of the human will (even in nominally Christian communities).

The opening to this collect recalls the truth of our situation to the mind of the believer—"we have no power in ourselves to help ourselves."

Despite the perceived advances in medicine, technology, safety procedures, or other things that we can do or use to attempt to extend our lives or protect against calamity, in the end, we have no true power to stave off injury, illness, and eventual death.

Left to our own devices, we may make strides in temporarily staving off mortal conditions, but we have no power or ability to give or restore life. Left to our own devices, we bring only ruin and desolation to our own souls, as we exalt the god of our will over the God of the universe.

To begin to approach the divinity of God and truly ask for His help and protection, we must first freely admit that we have no power to provide that help and protection for ourselves.

Asking for Protection

From this admission, the collect moves to two linked petitions which address the need for protection from outward harm and inward assaults.

"Keep us both outwardly in our bodies and inwardly in our souls" confronts head-on the facts of our creation, that we are both spirit and flesh. Asking God to "keep" us in our bodies and souls affirms that he made both good, and that we rely on him to preserve us in that state, acknowledging that without him our flesh decays and our souls wander into damnation.

The close of the petition clarifies to us what we are asking for: we ask for deliverance from physical injury and illness ("adversities which may happen to the body") and defense against the unseen powers which seek to assail our faith and lead us away from obedience to God's will for our lives ("evil thoughts which may assault and hurt the soul").

The closing address names the Lord of our lives as the defender of our bodies and souls. Since it is the Word of God by which all that exists was created, it is also by this Word that all continues to exist, and those who call upon that Word receive continual sustenance by the Holy Spirit, submitting their lives to the sovereignty of the Father and the oneness of the eternal God.

The Third Sunday in Lent *By Joshua Steele*

Heavenly Father, you have made us for yourself, and our hearts are restless until they rest in you: Look with compassion upon the heartfelt desires of your servants, and purify our disordered affections, that we may behold your eternal glory in the face of Christ Jesus; who lives and reigns with you and the Holy Spirit, one God, for ever and ever. Amen.

You have made us for yourself, and our hearts are restless until they rest in you

The opening of our collect this week comes straight from St. Augustine's *Confessions*, Book One, Chapter 1. In fact, here's the entirety of Chapter 1, which can really stand by itself as a reflection on the relationship between praising and invoking (calling upon) God:

> *Great art thou, O Lord, and greatly to be praised; great is thy power, and infinite is thy wisdom." And man desires to praise thee, for he is a part of thy creation; he bears his mortality about with him and carries the evidence of his sin and the proof that thou dost resist the proud. Still he desires to praise thee, this man who is only a small part of thy creation. Thou hast prompted him, that he should delight to praise thee,* ***for thou hast made us for thyself and restless is our heart until it comes to rest in thee.***
>
> *Grant me, O Lord, to know and understand whether first to invoke thee or to praise thee; whether first to know thee or call upon thee.*
>
> *But who can invoke thee, knowing thee not? For he who knows thee not may invoke thee as another than thou art. It may be that we should invoke thee in*

> *order that we may come to know thee. But "how shall they call on him in whom they have not believed? Or how shall they believe without a preacher?" Now, "they shall praise the Lord who seek him," for "those who seek shall find him," and, finding him, shall praise him.*
>
> *I will seek thee, O Lord, and call upon thee. I call upon thee, O Lord, in my faith which thou hast given me, which thou hast inspired in me through the humanity of thy Son, and through the ministry of thy preacher.*

I cannot really say it any better than St. Augustine did. We were created to delight in praising God. Our prayer life should, therefore, involve a mixture of praise, thanksgiving, and intercession/invocation.

Look with compassion upon the heartfelt desires of your servants,

God created our hearts, and he knows them even better than we do! It's therefore pointless to try and *hide* our heartfelt desires from the Lord, especially when we pray to him.

One of the great privileges of prayer is that we can be perfectly honest with God about what it is that our hearts desire. And, when we (frequently) realize that the desires of our hearts are insufficient or amiss, we can ask God to change the desires of our hearts! We can ask him to shape us, so that we might increasingly hate what he hates and love what he loves.

and purify our disordered affections, that we may behold your eternal glory in the face of Christ Jesus

Our restless hearts desire the wrong things. This is what it means to have "disordered affections." However, although this disorder affects every area of human life, God can, does, and will rightly order the affections of human hearts.

When the desires of our hearts are sanctified by the person and power of the Holy Spirit, we can pray to God knowing that he delights to grant us our heartfelt desires. God is not a stingy Father. He takes joy in meeting the needs of his children!

Finally, notice the goal of having rightly ordered affections—beholding the eternal glory of God in the face of Christ Jesus. After all, as Jesus declared in the Beatitudes, "Blessed are the pure in heart, for they shall see God" (Matt. 5:8). Or, as St. Paul says in 2 Corinthians 3:18 (NRSV), "And all of us, with unveiled faces, seeing the glory of the Lord as though reflected in a mirror, are being transformed into the same image from one degree of glory to another; for this comes from the Lord, the Spirit."

In this week's collect, we ask God to purify our hearts, that we might see him more clearly even now, in anticipation of beholding him face to face for all eternity.

The Fourth Sunday in Lent

By Michael Rosengren

Gracious Father, whose blessed Son Jesus Christ came down from heaven to be the true bread which gives life to the world: Evermore give us this bread, that he may live in us, and we in him; who lives and reigns with you and the Holy Spirit, one God, now and for ever. Amen.

"Jesus said to them, 'I am the bread of life; whoever comes to me shall not hunger, and whoever believes in me shall never thirst. But I said to you that you have seen me and yet do not believe.'" (John 6:35–36, ESV)

Physical Hunger and Spiritual Hunger

One of my favorite foods is fresh bread, especially when it is brought to you at your table at a restaurant. It smells so good and the butter melts right into the bread. Oh, it is so good. I have to be careful not to eat too much.

This is what is going on with Jesus and the crowd who had witnessed a miracle. Jesus made the bread and fish to be multiplied to feed thousands and there was some left over. WOW! But now the people wanted Jesus to do it again to feed their physical beings.

Their physical hunger was one thing, but Jesus knew their spiritual hunger was serious. The people didn't get it.

They wanted more physical bread, but not Jesus. Then Jesus declared the third "I am," or *ego eimi.* "I am the bread of life!" Jesus did not come down from heaven to provide only physical bread, but also the bread of life for the whole world.

Bread was the basic stuff of life in that day. The people Jesus spoke to knew that they could not live without their daily bread. So Jesus used this symbol of bread to teach them about their spiritual need.

What bread is for the body,
Jesus Christ is for our hungry,
aching hearts.

He alone can satisfy this deep spiritual hunger inside of us. Just as he didn't do another miracle to provide more physical bread, so too he doesn't want to ease our hurts and heartaches with quick-fix solutions. He wants to heal us deeper at the real source of our emotional pain.

How does Jesus heal us at the deepest level of our being? He proclaimed, "I am the true bread that the Father gives you from heaven. I came down from heaven to give life to the world." Looking at this claim in the context of this passage (John 6:51), we can discover the three ways that Jesus feeds our profound spiritual hunger and heals our deepest hurts. The true Bread of Life saves us, satisfies us, and strengthens us forevermore.

What are we hungry for?

In the season of Lent, we reflect and evaluate our lives in regard to our relationship with God as we prepare for Easter. What are we really hungry for? The true bread that came down from Heaven to give us abundant life? Or, are we hungry for the desires, appetites, and pleasures of this world which are only temporary like the manna in the Old Testament that lasted only one day?

Father, during this time of reflection, help us to hunger for the right thing. Help us to be present to the Presence in the present! Our spiritual hunger pangs are but our response to the aroma of the fresh bread of life that Christ has provided for us.

The Fifth Sunday in Lent *By Kolby Kerr*

Almighty God, you alone can bring into order the unruly wills and affections of sinners: Grant your people grace to love what you command and desire what you promise; that, among the swift and varied changes of this world, our hearts may surely there be fixed where true joys are to be found; through Jesus Christ our Lord, who lives and reigns with you and the Holy Spirit, one God, now and for ever. Amen.

The times, they are a-changin'.

Our home was built in the late 1950s, just as our city was beginning to sprawl out into suburban development. It's filled with large oaks that rain acorns down on the street, a thumping reminder of the humble, bygone origins of those trees.

Down the narrow hall, there's an anachronistic little installation. These days, we see it as a perfect shelf on which to set our laundry detergent, right across from the tiny closet that holds our stacked washer and dryer. But the shelf is too ornate for that. It's recessed into the wall of the hall and trimmed with white-washed wood. This was a central artery of the home back when it was built, because this was the telephone rack.

It's difficult to imagine what that must have been like, picking up the receiver, spinning the rotary dial, and then talking there, tethered to a shelf.

Yes. We know a thing or two about "swift and varied changes of this world." And it isn't merely the world that pulls the rug out from underneath us with its breakneck pace and supposed progress. The cares of our own lives spill out before us with an alarming fecundity. Why, in just walking down the hall to the telephone rack, I pass a bedroom with bunk beds where two boys snore out their gentle reminder that the times, they are a-changin'.

Like the breathless turning of the earth, time's flow rushes rampantly even when we sit still in its current. We cannot step out of the stream, and so we lose our bearings.

Which is why we need the declaration of this collect, with all its humbling bluntness.

The onslaught of our days warps our wills beyond our rule, bends our affections—like an eroded bend of a river around hard stone—toward our best guesses at what will bring us life. Usually, those best guesses have more to do with temporal convenience or comfort.

God alone stands out of time and shapes its bends. God alone can smooth its rapids. And so God alone can tame the wildness in our lives. Only God can fix our course, rudder our hearts from their short-sighted selfishness to everlasting hope—toward a country "where true joys are found."

Not that it's going to be pleasant. Like Eustace in C.S. Lewis's *The Voyage of the Dawn Treader*, our own *un-dragoning* isn't apt to feel nice. And chances are we will kick against our Father's guiding hands.

But if we have the eyes to see it, this is grace.

Grace to be wrenched from our own chaos into his rightly ordered command. Grace to stop chasing the enticements of the fleeting moment and to rest in his enduring promises.

Lent schools our desires. It forces us to feel the currents of our world, with all their swift and varied changes. And, if we allow ourselves to look to the horizon, Lent raises us up just enough to glimpse the land of true joys—the country where tombs are empty, where a table has been set, where someone has saved a place for us.

Holy Week

Palm Sunday *By Joshua Steele*

Almighty and everliving God, in your tender love for the human race you sent your Son our Savior Jesus Christ to take upon himself our nature, and to suffer death upon the Cross, giving us the example of his great humility: Mercifully grant that we may walk in the way of his suffering, and come to share in his resurrection; through Jesus Christ our Lord, who lives and reigns with you and the Holy Spirit, one God, for ever and ever. Amen.

Palm Sunday is an extremely significant liturgical moment within the Church year. The majority of Lent is behind us, and as we look ahead to Holy Week, a transformation takes place.

On Palm Sunday, the cries of "Hosanna!" are still ringing in our ears from the Procession of the Palms (see Matt. 21:1–11; Mark 11:1–11; Luke 19:29–40) as we hear the bloodthirsty shout: "Crucify him!" in our Gospel Lesson (Matt. 27:1–54; Mark 15:1–39; Luke 23:1–49).

"God, save us!" (the meaning of "Hosanna") becomes "God, damn him!" "May Christ be blessed!" becomes "May Christ be cursed!," for "cursed is everyone who is hanged on a tree" (Gal. 3:13; Deut. 21:23). The excited waving of supple palm branches becomes the bloodstained wood of a Roman cross.

A painful transition? Certainly. A necessary reflection? Even more so! This poignant combination of triumphal entry and crucifixion prepares us to live the Holy Week ahead, and the entirety of our lives, in the shadow of Christ's cross.

German theologian Jürgen Moltmann puts it well: "At the centre of Christian faith is the history of Christ. At the centre of the history of Christ is his passion and his death on the cross" (*The Way of Jesus Christ*, 151). There's no escaping it! You can have moralism or religiosity without a cross, but you cannot have a cross-less Christianity.

Almighty and everliving God, in your tender love for the human race you sent your Son our Savior Jesus Christ to take upon himself our nature, and to suffer death upon the cross, giving us the example of his great humility

As Christians, we follow a CRUCIFIED-and-Risen Messiah. This is not to deny the oft-neglected significance of the Resurrection, but it is a reminder that the empty tomb only has salvific significance to the extent that from it a once-DEAD man emerged! There's no escaping it. And as we prepare for Easter, we do well to remember that our celebrations of the Resurrection will only be as rich as our reflections upon the Cross.

As our collect reminds us, the Cross reminds us of the following:

- God loves us, tenderly.
- God's love for us motivated him to become one of us at the Incarnation.
- God's love for us motivated him to die for us at the Crucifixion.

Furthermore, at the Cross, Jesus Christ gives us the example of his great humility.

Philippians 2:1–11

Consider the words of St. Paul in Philippians 2:1–11 (ESV). Paul begins with Christian humility in verses 1–4:

> *So if there is any encouragement in Christ, any comfort from love, any participation in the Spirit, any affection and sympathy, complete my joy by being of the same mind, having the same love, being in full accord and of one mind. Do nothing from selfish ambition or conceit, but in humility count others more significant than yourselves. Let each of you look not only to his own interests, but also to the interests of others.*

Christian humility rests upon the humility of Jesus Christ, as demonstrated in the Incarnation and Crucifixion. Verses 5–8 read:

> *Have this mind among yourselves, which is yours in Christ Jesus, who, though he was in the form of God, did not count equality with God a thing to be grasped, but emptied himself, by taking the form of a servant, being born in the likeness of men. And being found in human form, he humbled himself by becoming obedient to the point of death, even death on a cross.*

Of course, that's not the end of the passage, however! Verses 9–11 read:

Therefore God has highly exalted him and bestowed on him the name that is above every name, so that at the name of Jesus every knee should bow, in heaven and on earth and under the earth, and every tongue confess that Jesus Christ is Lord, to the glory of God the Father.

Mercifully grant that we may walk in the way of his suffering, and also share in his resurrection

If Christian humility is only possible through the humility and humiliation of Jesus Christ, so too Christian resurrection and exaltation are only possible through the resurrection and exaltation of Jesus Christ. There is no resurrection, there is no exaltation, without the humiliation of the Crucifixion. No Easter without Good Friday. That is why we pray in the collect that we might be mercifully (!) enabled to walk in the way of Christ's suffering. It is so that we might also be mercifully enabled to share in the resurrection.

How are we called to walk in the way of Christ's suffering this Holy Week?

Let's consider this question as we work our way through the upcoming Holy Week. How and where is God calling us to die to ourselves and suffer for his glory?

Monday of Holy Week *By Jack King*

Almighty God, whose most dear Son went not up to joy but first he suffered pain, and entered not into glory before he was crucified: Mercifully grant that we, walking in the way of the Cross, may find it none other than the way of life and peace; through Jesus Christ your Son our Lord, who lives and reigns with you and the Holy Spirit, one God, for ever and ever. Amen.

"There's no excuse for not praying for your wife and children every single day."

I'll never forget this exhortation my spiritual director gave me several years ago. I already knew the importance of praying for my family, but I needed someone to awaken my heart to this crucial calling of prayer as a father. Ever since, I've sought to practice, learn, and grow in the way I pray over my family.

Many days I pray for specific situations and needs that my wife and kids will face. But over the years, I've gravitated to another pattern of intercessions over my family. When I'm only focused on the needs of the present moment, my prayers lack vision and insight of God's will for my family. Instead of limiting my prayers to specific needs, I take verses and phrases from Scripture to intercede for my family. As my 2-year-old son grows each day, I often pray that he would "grow in wisdom and stature, in favor with God and man"

(Luke 2:52). As I pray the psalms in the Daily Office, I often find a phrase that I will pray over my wife and daughter. "Send out your light and your truth, let them lead her to your holy hill and to your dwelling." (Psalm 43:3).

In recent months, I've also drawn on the beautiful collects in the Daily Office to intercede for my family. I've grown quite fond of the suggested daily rotation of collects in the ACNA's Morning and Evening Prayer services. I pray the collects in the sequence of Morning Prayer, but I return to them again during a time of free intercessions. On Mondays, I pray for my family that God would "guide our feet into the way of peace." On Wednesdays, I return to the phrase "that we may not fall into sin nor run into any danger" and offer this intercession for each person in my family.

A few Fridays ago, I was following this same practice of praying scripture and the daily collects, including Jesus' call to his disciples, "take up your cross and follow me," as a prayer over my family. The weekly collect for Friday is the same collect we pray on the Monday of Holy Week. It reminds us that every Friday is a commemoration of Good Friday. It directs me to pray that we would "walk in the way of the cross." And there in the ordinary rhythm of prayer that I've grown to know and love so well, I stopped speaking. I choked on the words.

Can I pray this for my family?

I love these three people with all my heart. I could not bear to think of the crosses that they will bear in this life. It's a harrowing thought to consider what the cross might mean in the lives of those we love. How can I pray this prayer over my children in the midst of their childlike innocence and joy? I want to delay this prayer, postpone it for as long as possible. They'll need their dad's prayer for endurance when they hit the cruelties of middle school life, but surely not when they're in preschool, right?

But then I have to face the denial in my heart that does not lead my family in the way of self-denial. I cannot pretend that the people I love most will somehow be exempt from suffering. I cannot deny that their faithfulness to Christ means carrying their own crosses. I want to do that for them, but I cannot. The Lord's call comes to each disciple, "If anyone would come after me, let him deny himself and take up his cross and follow me." I know I'm called to shoulder the burden of their cross, just as Simon of Cyrene walked with Jesus in the hour of our Lord's exhaustion. But even then, I cannot bring an end to their sufferings, present or future.

I have to face the truth of the cross for myself and for my family. But though I may finally be facing the truth about the cross for my family, I feel like another ancient father—Jacob—wrestling with God in a dark place (see Gen. 32:22–32). This prayer is no small moment in my life as a young father. God brought Jacob to Peniel for a reason, and God led me to the collect for Friday/Holy Monday for a reason. God led me here to see his truth anew. "God made foolish the wisdom of the world," which means the best wisdom for husbands and fathers in this world (and for all of us) is still foolishness without the cross. My best love for my family still needs to be baptized in the death and resurrection of Christ. Without the cross, I can only lead the people I love most to a finite and limited joy. With the cross, trusting in the "foolishness of the cross," I can draw on the strength and wisdom of God as I intercede for my family, praying that Christ would lead them to his infinite, unlimited joy.

The collect for Friday/Holy Monday as a way of life

Praying the cross over my family is a pivotal point, but I also know this is only the first test of many. It is not enough to pray this prayer once a year on Holy Monday—or even once a week on Friday. This is a prayer to be learned, memorized, and prayed for a lifetime. So also the prayers and words of the cross in intercession for my family. I train my mind, my soul, my heart—even my body—to pray this prayer so that when involuntary suffering comes to our family, I will remember the greatest truth about the cross—only the cross leads to "the way of life and peace."

I'm grateful that the collect for Friday/Holy Monday implies a kind of pilgrimage, a search. It is both a personal and communal search. We ask God, "Mercifully grant that we, walking in the way of the cross, may find it none other than the way of life and peace." I suppose each family is that little church where we help, encourage, and pray for one another to find that the way of the cross is truly the only way of life and peace.

In my life as a father, it's not enough to preach that Gospel on Sunday morning. It means preaching that Gospel to myself, praying that Gospel habitually so that I believe it in the depths of my heart, not for myself alone, but also for those I love most. Fridays may be like Peniel for the rest of my life and maybe they ought to be. But I take comfort that Peniel was the place Jacob could say he saw the face of God. And to see the face of the heavenly Father is to face a love who freely gave his only begotten Son so that all men, women, and children would be saved.

Tuesday of Holy Week *By Michael Matlock*

O Lord our God, whose blessed Son gave his back to be whipped and did not hide his face from shame and spitting: Give us grace to accept joyfully the sufferings of the present time, confident of the glory that shall be revealed; through Jesus Christ our Lord, who lives and reigns with you and the Holy Spirit, one God, for ever and ever. Amen.

The issue of suffering has been at the heart of the human quest for meaning.

Russian Orthodox Bishop Alexander Mileant says in a missionary pamphlet, "Afflictions in Our Lives," that

> daily, our life convinces us that sorrows are inevitable. Some suffer from need, some from the loss of loved ones, some from illness, some from slander and human malice, and some are tormented by their own passions, shortcomings or mistrust. Sometimes a person appears to be happy, but in reality, while experiencing torments of the soul, he is hiding his sorrows.

On this Tuesday of Holy Week, we pray to the Father for the capacity to suffer for the cause of righteousness. In this collect we hear clear echoes of St. Peter's instructions to Christians in exile: "B*ut rejoice insofar as you share Christ's sufferings, that you may also rejoice and be glad when his glory is revealed*" (1 Peter 4:13, ESV).

As Christ's disciples, we ask our Father that we may accompany Jesus in the Passion.

But perhaps you are like me. My feelings of faithful love can grow cold at times. I am not entirely fired with passion by the love of Jesus. So it is necessary for the health of my spirituality to pray for clearer vision and unobstructed hearing for Christ's love through every suffering of his Passion. I have to pray for God to develop in me a greater openness and readiness for change. "Lord, I honestly don't want to suffer right now. Please help me to change this attitude." If I try to change myself through my own efforts, I come up short. Therefore, I find it helpful to say often a slogan I have learned in Twelve Step Recovery Programs, "I can't, God can. Let him."

With St. Paul of the Cross (founder of the Passionists in the 18th century), let us petition our Lord that his most holy wounds be our delights and that we can keep him company in the Garden of Gethsemane. We can entreat our Lord that we gain the will to carry the tears of Jesus in the bosom of our souls, with great love and sorrow.

Because of our tragic fall from God, our turning away from our Heavenly Father, we have been led down a road to the depraved direction of our wills.

This depravity is the source of all humanity's sufferings and miseries. Diseases, sorrows, and physical death have arisen from moral evil.

Out of Israel's experience, a constant conviction emerges that God's people experience happiness and solace because of God's favor. On the other hand, their afflictions emerge from their own trespasses and from the wickedness of others, a kind of punishment for sins as a form of "revenge" for disobedience. Yet, the Old Testament Scriptures do present a counter notion of vicarious suffering on the part of the innocent servant, Israel, particularly in Isaiah 52:13–53:12. Sometimes God's people suffer not because of sin but even while remaining innocent.

Foremost in the New Testament is the notion that our redemption comes by the voluntary sufferings of the incarnate Son of God. These sufferings are not simply a retaliation for a trespass; they have an active redemptive power. Drawing from Bishop Alexander once again, he reminds us that "suffering is the fountain of renewal and salvation. God does not hide beyond the boundaries of vast space and He is not indifferent to humankind's misfortunes, as once thought the pagan wise men. On the contrary, He '*so loved the world that He gave His only begotten Son, that whosoever believes in Him should not perish but have everlasting life.*' (John 3:16)"

C. S. Lewis declares in *A Grief Observed* that we too are promised sufferings just as our Lord Christ endured. With penetrating incisiveness, he says that

> sufferings were part of the program. We were even told, *Blessed are they that mourn*, and I accept it. I've got nothing that I hadn't bargained for. Of course it is different when the thing happens to oneself, not to others, and in reality, not imagination.

Why does God allow us to suffer?

But part of my struggle, and perhaps yours, is with reconciling how a loving God invites and exhorts me to suffer. Again, let us hear from Lewis, but this time from *The Problem of Pain*:

> The problem of reconciling human suffering with the existence of a God who loves, is only insoluble so long as we attach a trivial meaning to the word "love," and look on things as if man were the centre of them. Man is not the centre. God does not exist for the sake of man. Man does not exist for his own sake. *Thou hast created all things, and for thy pleasure they are and were created.* We were made not primarily that we may love God (though we were made for that too) but that God may love us, that we may become objects in which the divine love may rest "well pleased."

One of the great saints of the Syrian Church from the 4th century, St. Ephrem, gives us wise counsel on dealing with suffering and affliction. Listen to him.

> Can you not endure insults? Keep quiet and you will be calmed. Do not think that you are suffering more than others. Just as one living on earth cannot escape the air, so it is impossible for a person living in this world not to be tempted by afflictions and disease. Those occupied with the earthly from the earthly—experience afflictions, whereas those aspiring towards spirituality about the spiritual suffer with the soul. However, the latter will be blessed because their fruit has been plentiful concerning God.

When afflictions or difficult circumstances occur, we shall with humility and patience await relief and help from

God, so that we would not be depressed with the thought that there is no hope of salvation for us. As we endure the sufferings and hardships that come our way as Jesus' followers, let us believe that these tribulations have lost their acuteness and darkness because of Christ's power of redemption in us. For the resurrected Christ is in us, and he is the hope of glory that surely includes our own resurrection.

Wednesday of Holy Week

By Joshua Steele

Assist us mercifully with your grace, Lord God of our salvation, that we may enter with joy upon the meditation of those mighty acts by which you have promised us life and immortality; through Jesus Christ our Lord, who lives and reigns with you and the Holy Spirit, one God, for ever and ever. Amen.

If you've ever had a horrendous Holy Week, then this collect is for you! It acknowledges that we need God's mercy and grace in order to observe Holy Week joyfully and contemplatively.

Otherwise, if we try to do Holy Week on our own, we will get distracted and bitter. The Maundy Thursday service will drag on. Good Friday and Holy Saturday will interfere with our weekend plans. And spending time with family after church on Easter Sunday will wear our patience thin.

LENT

Meditation upon the mighty acts of God is hard work. Joyful meditation is even harder. And, of course, this isn't just the case during Holy Week! For this reason, the following prayers from the Occasional Prayers in the 2019 *Book of Common Prayer* are especially helpful in broadening the collect for Holy Wednesday to include our everyday times of prayer, Scripture reading, and worship.

(97. Preparation for Personal Prayer)
Holy Spirit, breath of God and fire of love, I cannot pray without your aid: Kindle in me the fire of your love, and illumine me with your light; that with a steadfast will and holy thoughts I may approach the Father in spirit and in truth; through Jesus Christ my Lord, who reigns with you and the Father in eternal union. Amen.

(101. Before the Reading of Scripture)
Blessed Lord, who caused all Holy Scriptures to be written for our learning: Grant us so to hear them, read, mark, learn, and inwardly digest them, that by patience and the comfort of your Holy Word we may embrace and ever hold fast the blessed hope of everlasting life, which you have given us in our Savior Jesus Christ; who lives and reigns with you and the Holy Spirit, one God, for ever and ever. Amen.

(103. Preparation for Public Worship)
Guide and direct us, O Lord, always and everywhere with your holy light, that we may discern with clear vision your presence among us and partake with worthy intention of your divine mysteries. We ask this for Jesus Christ's sake. Amen.

This Holy Wednesday (and every time we approach the Lord in prayer and worship), let's swallow our pride and admit that we need God's help. And we don't just need it for the big things like salvation from Sin and Death. We need God's help just as much for the little things like paying joyful attention during the second half of Holy Week.

Maundy Thursday *By Myles Hixson*

Almighty Father, whose most dear Son, on the night before he suffered, instituted the Sacrament of his Body and Blood: Mercifully grant that we may receive it in thankful remembrance of Jesus Christ our Savior, who in these holy mysteries gives us a pledge of eternal life; and who lives and reigns with you and the Holy Spirit, one God, for ever and ever. Amen.

How do I know that I'm saved?

This is a question that plagues many faithful Christians, particularly those in Evangelical circles. With such a strong emphasis on a *personal* relationship with Jesus Christ, Evangelicalism has contributed to a false mindset in which salvation depends upon a person's *sense* of being saved. If I do not *feel* Jesus today—if I do not *feel* all that saved—then how do I know that I really am saved? If only there were something outside of my personal feelings that revealed God's love to me!

Thanks be to God, there is.

The Eucharist, Holy Communion

In the Collect for Maundy Thursday, we praise God for Christ's institution of the Blessed Sacrament, and we ask that we might receive it "thankfully in remembrance of Jesus Christ our Lord."
Why are we thankful for this Sacrament? Because through it God gives us a "pledge of eternal life." That little piece of bread and small sip of wine are his eternal promise that salvation is for us. If we receive those elements with faith, then we receive something that our feelings and consciousness can never produce, *assurance of salvation*.

But how? How can bread and wine do such a wonderful thing?

They cannot, but Christ can. Christ alone has earned eternity through his perfect life, death, and resurrection. For us to be saved, we must become partakers of his life. We must be united to his perfection, so that our sinfulness can be forgiven and overcome by his grace.

In the Eucharist, this is exactly what happens. His precious, spotless, blameless Body and Blood are made present and given to us mystically but no less fully. He is real. He is there. His Body enters into our body. His Blood mingles with our blood. And through this "holy mystery" the two "become one flesh" (Eph. 5:31–32). What belongs to him (eternal life) becomes ours. What belongs to us (sin and death) is taken away by him and his sacrifice.

It is here, at the Eucharist, that we find salvation— a salvation that frees us from subjectivity and the oppression of our own emotions.

Because of the Eucharist, we do not have to worry about feeling Jesus enough to be saved; we will never feel him enough. Because of the Eucharist, we do not have to worry about having enough faith; we will never have enough faith. Because of the Eucharist, we are free to trust in Christ alone and to firmly believe that the bread and the wine is "given for us" (Luke 22:19).

How do I know that I'm saved? Do not fall into the trap of pointing to your feelings or experience to answer this question. Point to the altar instead. Point to Christ. He will save you.

Good Friday *By Kolby Kerr*

Almighty God, we beseech you graciously to behold this your family, for whom our Lord Jesus Christ was willing to be betrayed and given into the hands of sinners, and to suffer death upon the Cross; who now lives and reigns with you and the Holy Spirit, one God, for ever and ever. Amen.

Asking God

Every collect makes a request. After all, the essential act of any prayer is *asking*. This may at first seem selfish—*should not prayer be about giving thanks?* But remember Jesus' parable of the Pharisee and the tax collector (Luke 18:9–14). The Pharisee's prayer was one of thanks: namely, he thanked God that he wasn't like all those other sinners over there (especially that disgusting tax collector!). The tax collector's prayer was a request: "God, be merciful to me!"

Asking always begins with an admission of our insufficiency. We are brought back down to our proper place as children, which is precisely the posture God desires (as Jesus outlines in Matt. 7:7–11). This is why the Psalms are always asking, even pleading—hear me, save me, draw near to me, etc.

"Behold This Your Family"

So what does this Good Friday collect ask of God? It's a stunningly simple request: "...behold this your family..." In this holy moment, this darkest of days, we ask God in his love and grace to see us, to hold us in his sight.

The request is as essential as it is simple, because at the core of our being, isn't this what we are looking for? To be seen, to be known, to belong, to be held. Also, notice that this request to be seen isn't relegated to the purely personal. The request is for all of us—the gathered community of worshipers. We do not single out ourselves for special notice.

The Family of Jesus Christ

The simplicity of the request here belies a complex and wonderful truth. We are only enabled to ask to be seen, identified, and esteemed by God as his family through saving work of Jesus. As Paul says in Romans 8:12–17, it is our status as God's *adopted* children that allows us to cry "*Abba, Father!*"

The collect rehearses the escalating awfulness of the path Christ took, emphasizing his *willingness* to be betrayed by those closest to him, delivered over to those who misunderstood and despised him, and, at last, to suffer the cruelty of the cross. The willingness of Christ so poignantly expressed in Jesus' prayer in the garden of Gethsemane (Matt. 26:36–46; Mark 14:32–42; Luke 22:40–46), affirms the never-failing love of God.

A Plain Good Friday

There are fewer collects as plain and unadorned as this. There will be a season for overflowing rhetoric, abounding imagery, and grand requests. But this plainness fits this day. On Good Friday, we are suspended for the briefest moments in hopelessness. We find ourselves in darkness, not certain if any sun shall ever rise.

And so we pray not for eyes to see, but rather to be seen. As we recall Jesus' suffering upon the cross, we remember that we are seen by God because Christ was willing to be forsaken.

Holy Saturday and the Easter Vigil

By Gerald R. McDermott

Holy Saturday

O God, Creator of heaven and earth: Grant that, as the crucified body of your dear Son was laid in the tomb and rested on this holy Sabbath, so we may await with him the coming of the third day, and rise with him to newness of life; through Jesus Christ our Lord. Amen.

or this

O God of the living, on this day your Son our Savior descended to the place of the dead: Look with kindness on all of us who wait in hope for liberation from the corruption of sin and death, and give us a share in the glory of the children of God; through Jesus Christ your Son our Lord. Amen.

Holy Saturday is one of those great mysteries that the early church pondered.

What was Christ doing between his death and resurrection (in his divinity rather than his humanity)? What did the creed mean by Jesus having "descended to the dead"? Is this what Peter meant when he wrote that Jesus "preached to the spirits in prison" (1 Pet. 3:19)? What happened to the souls of all those who lived before the Incarnation and never heard the gospel?

Holy Saturday was the answer to all these questions.

Tertullian wrote that Christ descended to Hades (the upper portion of Sheol) on Holy Saturday to acquaint the patriarchs and prophets with his redeeming mission.

Cyril of Alexandria preached that Christ appeared to all those in the "lower regions" (Eph 4:9) so that they too could benefit from his coming. "The only-begotten Son shouted with authority to the suffering souls, saying to those in chains, 'Come out!' and to those in darkness, 'Be enlightened!'" Some believed and were freed. Others, blinded by idolatry or lusts, could not see him and so were not delivered. This was the "harrowing of hell" that the medieval church celebrated in its pageants.

Whether we believe the early church got 1 Peter 3 right or not, we can take its interpretation as a symbol of their conviction—and that of the Great Tradition—that God is just and loving and will deal accordingly with all those who have not heard.

Easter Vigil/Eve

O God, you made this most holy night to shine with the glory of the Lord's resurrection: Stir up in your Church that Spirit of adoption which is given to us in Baptism, that we, being renewed both in body and mind, may worship you in sincerity and truth; through Jesus Christ our Lord, who lives and reigns with you, in the unity of the Holy Spirit, one God, now and for ever. Amen.

The Easter Vigil is the greatest service of the Christian year.

Augustine called it "the mother of all vigils." Just as Jews believe in their Passover seder that they are brought back into the original event of redemption so that they become contemporaries of it, so too the historic Church has believed that in this "Great Sabbath" time, especially its Bible readings recounting the history of salvation, the faithful participate in these events as contemporaries.

When they are sprinkled with water, Christians are lifted up out of linear time into sacramental time to join Christ in his baptism, both by water and blood. Then at its climax—the Eucharist—they are joined to the risen Christ in his humanity and not only his divinity. The resurrection of their Lord is no longer a past event but a present reality. Because the service starts in darkness and ends with light, they can recite the collect with joy and fresh recognition: "O God, you made this holy night to shine with the glory of the Lord's resurrection."

Easter Sunday *By Joshua Steele*

Almighty God, who through your only-begotten Son Jesus Christ overcame death and opened to us the gate of everlasting life: Grant that we, who celebrate with joy the day of the Lord's resurrection, may, by your life-giving Spirit, be delivered from sin and raised from death; through Jesus

Christ our Lord, who lives and reigns with you and the Holy Spirit, one God, now and for ever. Amen.

Or this

O God, who for our redemption gave your only-begotten Son to die upon the Cross, and by his glorious resurrection delivered us from the devil and the power of death: Grant us grace to die daily to sin, that we may live with him in the joy of his resurrection; who lives and reigns with you and the Holy Spirit, now and for ever. Amen.

There are actually two collects for Easter Sunday.

First, let's consider what both collects say about God.

"Almighty God, who through your only-begotten Son Jesus Christ overcame death and opened to us the gate of everlasting life:"

The good news of the gospel is the good news of God's rescue mission. Having created the universe to be a realm of perfect relationships, between (1) God and humans, (2) humans and each other, and (3) humans and the rest of creation (see Genesis 1–2), God was not content to let Sin and Death, which infected and affected every layer of the universe (see Genesis 3), have the final word.

No, instead, God puts the universe back together again,

chiefly and ultimately through the life, death, and RESURRECTION of Jesus Christ, the eternal Son of God. The Resurrection, then, is the monument of God's victory over Sin and Death. It is also, as the first Easter Collect notes, the "gate of everlasting life." That is, the Resurrection is not just an afterthought to the gospel—mere proof that the Cross "worked." It is much more. It is the first and final victory over Death, our ancient foe.

"O God, who for our redemption gave your only-begotten Son to die upon the cross, and by his glorious resurrection delivered us from the power of death and the devil:"

As the second Easter Collect notes, it was/is through the Resurrection that God delivers us from "the power of death and the devil." I love this collect because it draws my attention to aspects of the atonement which were underemphasized in my own upbringing. I grew up hearing about the gospel chiefly in financial and/or judicial terms—"penal substitutionary atonement," as it's called. Jesus Christ died to pay my debt. He died in my stead, to take my guilt upon himself, so that I might be declared righteous in his stead. A beautiful exchange. And, in my opinion, a very important and true facet of the gospel!

But there's more to the gospel than just penal substitutionary atonement. This second Easter Collect recalls what are known as "Christus Victor" and "Ransom" theories of the atonement—ways of explaining the gospel that emphasize Christ's cosmic victory over Sin and Death, in order to liberate us, his people, from our bondage. A glorious victory. That's what we celebrate at Easter!

Then, let's consider what both collects actually pray for.

Allow me to take the editorial liberty of putting the petitions of both collects together:

> 1. *"Grant that we, who celebrate with joy the day of the Lord's resurrection, may be raised from the death of sin by your life-giving Spirit."*
>
> 2. *"Grant us the grace to die daily to sin, that we may live with him in the joy of his resurrection."*

Would you look at that! We've created a "collect chiasm," as it were! The petitions of both prayers together move from:

- JOY to
- DYING TO SIN to
- DYING TO SIN to
- JOY again.

This Easter, we ask God to give us JOY as we celebrate the Resurrection.

Sure, we live in a world that is still stained by Sin and often, it appears, dominated by Death. However, on Easter Sunday (and on EVERY Sunday!), we remind ourselves that Sin and Death have lost the battle. We know how God's Story ends—with Resurrection and eternal life! So, on that basis, we ask God to give us his joy, even in the midst of our earthly sorrows.

This Easter, we ask God to help us to DIE TO SIN through the power of the Holy Spirit.

It simply will. Not. Do. To celebrate the Resurrection with our lips, and yet deny the Resurrection with our lives. We ought not to celebrate our deliverance from bondage to Sin and Death as we demonstrate our captivity to Sin and Death! In order to experience the liberating results of the Resurrection, we need the Holy Spirit to change us from the inside out—so that we might hate what God hates and love what God loves. Easter Sunday isn't just a "feel-good" moment, it's a life-transforming moment.

Has Jesus Christ set you free from bondage to Sin and Death? Then be joyful and die daily to sin.

APPENDIX A

Lenten Lectionary Readings: Scripture for the Journey

A LECTIONARY is simply a list of Scripture readings. In the Anglican tradition, there are lectionaries for daily use in Morning and Evening Prayer (Daily Office Lectionaries) and for use in the church's main worship services of Holy Communion (Sunday and Holy Day Lectionaries).

(For more information on using a lectionary, see Winfield Bevins's "Using the Lectionary to Read Scripture in Lent" in chapter 2, p. 62.)

Sunday Readings

To guide your use of Scripture throughout Lent and Holy Week, we've provided the Sunday Lectionary readings from the Anglican Church in North America's (ACNA) 2019 *Book of Common Prayer*. Again, in the Anglican tradition, these readings are used during worship services of Holy Communion.

Note that this Sunday Lectionary is a three-year cycle of readings. Year A begins with Advent (in November–December) in those years evenly divisible by three. So, when you're observing Lent (in February–April), that means that, if the current year is divisible by three, you're in Year C. (Lent 2020 is Year A, Lent 2021 is Year B, and Lent 2022, divisible by three, is Year C. Lent 2023 is Year A again.)

Daily Readings

However, when it comes to Daily Office readings (for use at Morning and Evening Prayer), we've included the readings from the 1979 *Book of Common Prayer*, because they follow the liturgical calendar and the season of Lent. (To access the ACNA's 2019 BCP's Daily Office Lectionary, which follows the civil calendar, go to http://bcp2019.anglicanchurch.net/.)

Note that this Daily Office Lectionary is a two-year cycle of readings. Year One begins with Advent preceding odd-numbered years. So, when you're observing Lent, if the current year is odd-numbered, it's Year One. If it's even-numbered, Year Two.

As for the readings themselves, note that the first line for each day lists the Psalms, with those for the morning given first, followed by those for the evening. Then, on the second line are three readings for the day. You may use two readings in the morning and one in the evening. It's suggested to read the Gospel reading in the evening in Year One, and in the morning in Year Two. Or, if you're only praying once that day, you can read all three at that time.

Note: in both lectionaries, brackets and parentheses indicate optional readings

SUNDAY READINGS

DAY	YEAR A	YEAR B	YEAR C
LENT			
Ash Wedneday	Joel 2:1–2, 12–17 or Isa 58:1–12 Ps 103 or 103:8–14 2 Cor 5:20—6:10 Matt 6:1–6, 16–21		
1st Sunday	Gen 2:4–9, 15–17, 25—3:7 Ps 51 or Ps 51:1–12 Rom 5:12–21 Matt 4:1–11	Gen 9:8–17 Ps 25 or 25:3–9 1 Pet 3:18–22 Mark 1:9–13	Deut 26:(1–4)5–11 Ps 91 or 91:9–16 Rom 10:4–13 Luke 4:1–13
2nd Sunday	Gen 12:1–9 Ps 33:12–22 Rom 4:1–5(6–12)13–17 John 3:1–16	Gen 22:1–14 Ps 16 or 16:5–11 Rom 8:31–39 Mark 8:31–38	Gen 15:1–18 Ps 27 or 27:7–14 Phil 3:17—4:1 Luke 13:(22–30)31–35
3rd Sunday	Ex 17:1–7 Ps 95 Rom 1:16–32 John 4:5–26(27–38)39–42	Ex 20:1–21 Ps 19:7–14 Rom 7:12–25 John 2:13–22	Ex 3:1–15 Ps 103 or 103:1–12 1 Cor 10:1–13 Luke 13:1–9(10–17)
4th Sunday	1 Sam 16:1–13 Ps 23 Eph 5:1–14 John 9:1–13, 28–38(39–41)	2 Chr 36:14–23 Ps 122 Eph 2:1–10 John 6:1–15	Josh (4:19–24) 5:1(2–8) 9–12 Ps 34 or 34:1–8 2 Cor 5:17–21 Luke 15:11–32
5th Sunday (Passion)	Ezek 37:1–14 Ps 130 Rom 6:15–23 John 11:(1–17)18–44	Jer 31:31–34 Ps 51 or 51:10–15 Heb (4:14–16)5:1–10 John 12:20–33(34–36)	Isa 43:16–21 Ps 126 Phil 3:7–16 Luke 20:9–19
HOLY WEEK			
Liturgy of the Palms	Matt 21:1–11 Ps 118:19–29	Mark 11:1–11a Ps 118:19–29	Luke 19:29–40 Ps 118:19–29
Palm Sunday	Isa 52:13—53:12 Ps 22:1–21 or 22:1–11 Phil 2:5–11 Matt (26:36–75) 27:1–54 (55–66)	Isa 52:13—53:12 Ps 22:1–11 or 22:1–21 Phil 2:5–11 Mark (14:32–72)15:1–39 (40–47)	Isa 52:13—53:12 Ps 22:1–11 or 22:1–21 Phil 2:5–11 Luke (22:39–71) 23:1–49 (50–56)
Holy Monday	Isa 42:1–9 Ps 36:5–10 Heb 11:39—12:3 John 12:1–11 or Mark 14:3–9		
Holy Tuesday	Isa 49:1–6 Ps 71:1–12 1 Cor 1:18–31 John 12:37–38,42–50 or Mark 11:15–19		

<table>
<tr><td>Holy Wednesday</td><td colspan="3">Isa 50:4–9
Ps 69:6–13, 20–21
Heb 9:11–28
Matt 26:1–5,14–25</td></tr>
<tr><td>Maundy Thursday</td><td colspan="3">Ex 12:1–14
Ps 78:14–25
1 Cor 11:23–26 (27–34)
John 13:1–15 or Luke 22:14–30</td></tr>
<tr><td>Good Friday</td><td colspan="3">Gen 22:1–18 or Isa 52:13—53:12
Ps 22:1–11(12–21) or 40:1–13 or 69:1–21
Heb 10:1–25
John (18:1–40) 19:1–37</td></tr>
<tr><td>Holy Saturday</td><td colspan="3">Job 14:1–17
Ps 130 or 31:1–5
1 Pet 4:1–8
Matt 27:57–66 or John 19:38–42</td></tr>
<tr><td colspan="4">EASTER</td></tr>
<tr><td>Easter Vigil</td><td colspan="3">Gen 1:1—2:3
Gen 3
Gen 7:1–5,11–18; 8:6–20; 9:8–13
Gen 22:1–18
Ex 14:10—15:1
Isa 4:2–6
Isa 55:1–11
Ezek 36:24–28
Ezek 37:1–14
Dan 3:1–28
Jonah 1:1—2:10
Zeph 3:12–20
Rom 6:3–11
Matt 28:1–10</td></tr>
<tr><td>Easter: Early Service</td><td colspan="3">Use one of the Old Testament Lessons from the Easter Vigil
Ps 114
Rom 6:3–11
Matt 28:1–10</td></tr>
<tr><td>Easter: Main Service</td><td>Acts 10:34–43
or Ex 14:10–14, 21–31
Ps 118:14–17, 22–24
Col 3:1–4
or Acts 10:34–43
John 20:1–10 (11–18)
or Matt 28:1–10</td><td>Acts 10:34–43
or Isa 25:6–9
Ps 118:14–17 22–24
Col 3:1–4
or Acts 10:34–43
Mark 16:1–8</td><td>Acts 10:34–43
or Isa 51:9–11
Ps 118:14–17, 22–24
Col 3:1–4
or Acts 10:34–43
Luke 24:1–12</td></tr>
<tr><td>Easter: Evening Service</td><td colspan="3">Dan 12:1–3
Ps 136
1 Cor 5:6–8
Luke 24:13–35</td></tr>
</table>

DAILY READINGS IN ODD-NUMBERED YEARS (YEAR ONE)

Week of 1 Lent

Sunday	Pss 63:1–8(9–11), 98 ✣ 103		
	Deut 8:1–10	1 Cor 1:17–31	Mark 2:18–22
Monday	41, 52 ✣ 144		
	Deut 8:11–20	Heb 2:11–18	John 2:1–12
Tuesday	45 ✣ 47, 48		
	Deut 9:4–12	Heb 3:1–11	John 2:13–22
Wednesday	119:49–72 ✣ 49, [53]		
	Deut 9:13–21	Heb 3:12–19	John 2:23—3:15
Thursday	50 ✣ [59, 60] *or* 19, 46		
	Deut 9:23—10:5	Heb 4:1–10	John 3:16–21
Friday	95 & 40, 54 ✣ 51		
	Deut 10:12–22	Heb 4:11–16	John 3:22–36
Saturday	55 ✣ 138, 139:1–17(18–23)		
	Deut 11:18–28	Heb 5:1–10	John 4:1–26

Week of 2 Lent

Sunday	24, 29 ✣ 8, 84		
	Jer 1:1–10	1 Cor 3:11–23	Mark 3:31—4:9
Monday	56, 57, [58] ✣ 64, 65		
	Jer 1:11–19	Rom 1:1–15	John 4:27–42
Tuesday	61, 62 ✣ 68:1–20(21–23)24–36		
	Jer 2:1–13	Rom 1:16–25	John 4:43–54
Wednesday	72 119:73–96		
	Jer 3:6–18	Rom 1:28—2:11	John 5:1–18
Thursday	[70], 71 ✣ 74		
	Jer 4:9–10,19–28	Rom 2:12–24	John 5:19–29
Friday	95 & 69:1–23(24–30)31–38 ✣ 73		
	Jer 5:1–9	Rom 2:25—3:18	John 5:30–47
Saturday	75, 76 ✣ 23, 27		
	Jer 5:20–31	Rom 3:19–31	John 7:1–13

DAILY READINGS IN EVEN-NUMBERED YEARS (YEAR TWO)

Week of 1 Lent

Sunday	Pss 63:1–8(9–11), 98 ✣ 103		
	Dan 9:3–10	Heb 2:10–18	John 12:44–50
Monday	41, 52 ✣ 44		
	Gen 37:1–11	1 Cor 1:1–19	Mark 1:1–13
Tuesday	45 ✣ 47, 48		
	Gen 37:12–24	1 Cor 1:20–31	Mark 1:14–28
Wednesday	119:49–72 ✣ 49, [53]		
	Gen 37:25–36	1 Cor 2:1–13	Mark 1:29–45
Thursday	50 ✣ [59, 60] *or* 19, 46		
	Gen 39:1–23	1 Cor 2:14—3:15	Mark 2:1–12
Friday	95 & 40, 54 ✣ 51		
	Gen 40:1–23	1 Cor 3:16–23	Mark 2:13–22
Saturday	55 ✣ 138, 139:1–17(18–23)		
	Gen 41:1–13	1 Cor 4:1–7	Mark 2:23—3:6

Week of 2 Lent

Sunday	24, 29 ✣ 8, 84		
	Gen 41:14–45	Rom 6:3–14	John 5:19–24
Monday	56, 57, [58] ✣ 64, 65		
	Gen 41:46–57	1 Cor 4:8–20(21)	Mark 3:7–19a
Tuesday	61, 62 ✣ 68:1–20(21–23)24–36		
	Gen 42:1–17	1 Cor 5:1–8	Mark 3:19b–35
Wednesday	72 ✣ 119:73–96		
	Gen 42:18–28	1 Cor 5:9—6:8	Mark 4:1–20
Thursday	[70], 71 ✣ 74		
	Gen 42:29–38	1 Cor 6:12–30	Mark 4:21–34
Friday	95 & 69:1–23(24–30)31–38 ✣ 73		
	Gen 43:1–15	1 Cor 7:1–9	Mark 4:35–41
Saturday	75, 76 ✣ 23, 27		
	Gen 43:16–34	1 Cor 7:10–24	Mark 5:1–20

Week of 3 Lent

Sunday	Pss 93, 96 ✣ 34		
	Jer 6:9–15	1 Cor 6:12–20	Mark 5:1–20
Monday	80 ✣ 77, [79]		
	Jer 7:1–15	Rom 4:1–12	John 7:14–36
Tuesday	78:1–39 ✣ 78:40–72		
	Jer 7:21–34	Rom 4:13–25	John 7:37–52
Wednesday	119:97–120 ✣ 81, 82		
	Jer 8:18—9:6	Rom 5:1–11	John 8:12–20
Thursday	[83] *or* 42, 43 ✣ 85, 86		
	Jer 10:11–24	Rom 5:12–21	John 8:21–32
Friday	95 & 88 ✣ 91, 92		
	Jer 11:1–8,14–20	Rom 6:1–11	John 8:33–47
Saturday	87, 90 ✣ 136		
	Jer 13:1–11	Rom 6:12–23	John 8:47–59

Week of 4 Lent

Sunday	66, 67 ✣ 19, 46		
	Jer 14:1–9,17–22	Gal 4:21—5:1	Mark 8:11–21
Monday	89:1–18 ✣ 89:19–52		
	Jer 16:10–21	Rom 7:1–12	John 6:1–15
Tuesday	97, 99, [100] ✣ 94, [95]		
	Jer 17:19–27	Rom 7:13–25	John 6:16–27
Wednesday	101, 109:1–4(5–19)20–30 ✣ 119:121–144		
	Jer 18:1–11	Rom 8:1–11	John 6:27–40
Thursday	69:1–23(24–30)31–38 ✣ 73		
	Jer 22:13–23	Rom 8:12–27	John 6:41–51
Friday	95 & 102 ✣ 107:1–32		
	Jer 23:1–8	Rom 8:28–39	John 6:52–59
Saturday	107:33–43, 108:1–6(7–13) ✣ 33		
	Jer 23:9–15	Rom 9:1–18	John 6:60–71

Week of 3 Lent

Sunday	Pss 93, 96 ✣ 34		
	Gen 44:1–17	Rom 8:1–10	John 5:25–29
Monday	80 ✣ 77, [79]		
	Gen 44:18–34	1 Cor 7:25–31	Mark 5:21–43
Tuesday	78:1–39 ✣ 78:40–72		
	Gen 45:1–15	1 Cor 7:32–40	Mark 6:1–13
Wednesday	119:97–120 ✣ 81, 82		
	Gen 45:16–28	1 Cor 8:1–13	Mark 6:13–29
Thursday	[83] *or* 42, 43 ✣ 85, 86		
	Gen 46:1–7,28–34	1 Cor 9:1–15	Mark 6:30–46
Friday	95 & 88 ✣ 91, 92		
	Gen 47:1–26	1 Cor 9:16–27	Mark 6:47–56
Saturday	87, 90 ✣ 136		
	Gen 47:27—48:7	1 Cor 10:1–13	Mark 7:1–23

Week of 4 Lent

Sunday	66, 67 ✣ 19, 46		
	Gen 48:8–22	Rom 8:11–25	John 6:27–40
Monday	89:1–18 ✣ 89:19–52		
	Gen 49:1–28	1 Cor 10:14—11:1	Mark 7:24–37
Tuesday	97, 99, [100] ✣ 94, [95]		
	Gen 49:29—50:14	1 Cor 11:17–34	Mark 8:1–10
Wednesday	101, 109:1–4(5–19)20–30 ✣ 119:121–144		
	Gen 50:15–26	1 Cor 12:1–11	Mark 8:11–26
Thursday	69:1–23(24–30)31–38 ✣ 73		
	Exod 1:6–22	1 Cor 12:12–26	Mark 8:27—9:1
Friday	95 & 102 ✣ 107:1–321		
	Exod 2:1–22	Cor 12:27—13:3	Mark 9:2–13
Saturday	107:33–43, 108:1–6(7–13) ✣ 33		
	Exod 2:23—3:15	1 Cor 13:1–13	Mark 9:14–29

DAILY READINGS IN ODD-NUMBERED YEARS (YEAR ONE)

Week of 5 Lent

Sunday Ps 118 ✣ 145
Jer 23:16–32 1 Cor 9:19–27 Mark 8:31—9:1

Monday 31 ✣ 35
Jer 24:1–10 Rom 9:19–33 John 9:1–17

Tuesday [120], 121, 122, 123 ✣ 124, 125, 126, [127]
Jer 25:8–17 Rom 10:1–13 John 9:18–41

Wednesday 119:145–176 ✣ 128, 129, 130
Jer 25:30–38 Rom 10:14–21 John 10:1–18

Thursday 131, 132, [133] ✣ 140, 142
Jer 26:1–16 Rom 11:1–12 John 10:19–42

Friday 95 & 22 ✣ 141, 143:1–11(12)
Jer 29:1,4–13 Rom 11:13–24 John 11:1–27 *or* 12:1–10

Saturday 137:1–6(7–9), 144 ✣ 42, 43
Jer 31:27–34 Rom 11:25–36 John 11:28–44 *or* 12:37–50

Holy Week

Palm Sunday 24, 29 ✣ 103
Zech 9:9–12* 1 Tim 6:12–16*
Zech 12:9–11, 13:1,7–9** Matt 21:12–17**

Monday 51:1–18(19–20) ✣ 69:1–23
Jer 12:1–16 Phil 3:1–14 John 12:9–19

Tuesday 6, 12 ✣ 94
Jer 15:10–21 Phil 3:15–21 John 12:20–26

Wednesday 55 ✣ 74
Jer 17:5–10,14–17 Phil 4:1–13 John 12:27–36

Maundy Thursday 102 ✣ 142, 143
Jer 20:7–11 1 Cor 10:14–17, 11:27–32 John 17:1–11(12–26)

Good Friday 95 & 22 ✣ 40:1–14(15–19),54
Wisdom 1:16—2:1,12–22 1 Peter 1:10–20 John 13:36–38*
or Gen 22:1–14 John 19:38–42**

Holy Saturday 95* & 88 ✣ 27
Job 19:21–27a Heb 4:1–16* Rom 8:1–11**

Easter Day Pss 148, 149, 150 ✣ 113, 114, *or* 118
Exod 12:1–14* —— John 1:1–18*
Isa 51:9–11** Luke 24:13–35**, *or* John 20:19–23**

** Intended for use in the morning* *** Intended for use in the evening*

DAILY READINGS IN EVEN-NUMBERED YEARS (YEAR TWO)

Week of 5 Lent

Sunday Ps 118 ✣ 145
Exod 3:16—4:12 Rom 12:1–21 John 8:46–59

Monday 31 ✣ 35
Exod 4:10–20(21–26)27–31 1 Cor 14:1–19 Mark 9:30–41

Tuesday [120], 121, 122, 123 ✣ 124, 125, 126, [127]
Exod 5:1—6:1 1 Cor 14:20–33a,39–40 Mark 9:42–50

Wednesday 119:145–176 ✣ 128, 129, 130
Exod 7:8–24 2 Cor 2:14—3:6 Mark 10:1–16

Thursday 131, 132, [133] ✣ 140, 142
Exod 7:25—8:19 2 Cor 3:7–18 Mark 10:17–31

Friday 95 & 22 ✣ 141, 143:1–11(12)
Exod 9:13–35 2 Cor 4:1–12 Mark 10:32–45

Saturday 137:1–6(7–9), 144 ✣ 42, 43
Exod 10:21—11:8 2 Cor 4:13–18 Mark 10:46–52

Holy Week

Palm Sunday 24, 29 ✣ 103
Zech 9:9–12* 1 Tim 6:12–16*
Zech 12:9–11, 13:1,7–9** Luke 19:41–48**

Monday 51:1–18(19–20) ✣ 69:1–23
Lam 1:1–2,6–12 2 Cor 1:1–7 Mark 11:12–25

Tuesday 6, 12 ✣ 94
Lam 1:17–22 2 Cor 1:8–22 Mark 11:27–33

Wednesday 55 ✣ 4
Lam 2:1–9,14–17 2 Cor 1:23—2:11 Mark 12:1–11

Maundy Thursday 102 ✣ 142, 143
Lam 2:10–18 1 Cor 10:14–17, 11:27–32 Mark 14:12–25

Good Friday 95 & 22 ✣ 40:1–14(15–19),54
Lam 3:1–9, 19–33 1 Peter 1:10–20 John 13:36–38*
John 19:38–42**

Holy Saturday 95* & 88 ✣ 27
Lam 3:37–58 Heb 4:1–16* Rom 8:1–11**

Easter Day Pss 148, 149, 150 ✣ 113, 114, *or* 118
Exod 12:1–14* —— John 1:1–18*
Isa 51:9–11** Luke 24:13–35**, *or* John 20:19–23**

** Intended for use in the morning* *** Intended for use in the evening*

APPENDIX B

Recommended Lent Resources: Continue the Journey

- *Make Room: A Child's Guide to Lent and Easter*, by Laura Alary
- *A Way other than Our Own: Devotions for Lent*, by Walter Brueggemann
- *40 Days of Decrease: A Different Kind of Hunger. A Different Kind of Fast*, by Alicia Britt Chole
- *The Good of Giving Up: Discovering the Freedom of Lent*, by Aaron Damiani
- *The Common Rule: Habits of Purpose for an Age of Distraction*, by Justin Whitmel Earley
- *Celebration of Discipline: The Path to Spiritual Growth*, by Richard J. Foster
- *Pauses for Lent: 40 Words for 40 Days*, by Trevor Hudson
- *Bread and Wine: Readings for Lent and Easter*, readings from C.S. Lewis, G.K. Chesterton, and others.
- *Lent with the Desert Fathers*, by Thomas McKenzie
- *The Crucifixion: Understanding the Death of Jesus Christ*, by Fleming Rutledge

- *Three Hours: Sermons for Good Friday,* by Fleming Rutledge
- *Emotionally Healthy Spirituality: It's Impossible to Be Spiritually Mature, While Remaining Emotionally Immature,* by Peter Scazzero
- *Great Lent: Journey to Pascha,* by Alexander Schmemann
- *Soul Feast : An Invitation to the Christian Spiritual Life,* by Marjorie J. Thompson
- *Lent for Everyone: Matthew, Year A: A Daily Devotional,* by N.T. Wright
- *Lent for Everyone: Mark, Year B: A Daily Devotional,* by N.T. Wright
- *Lent for Everyone: Luke, Year C: A Daily Devotional,* by N.T. Wright

APPENDIX C

Contributors

Tish Harrison Warren is a priest in the Anglican Church in North America. She has worked in ministry settings for over a decade as a campus minister with InterVarsity Graduate and Faculty Ministries, as an associate rector, and with addicts and those in poverty through various churches and non-profit organizations. She is now Writer in Residence at Church of the Ascension in Pittsburgh, PA. She is the author of Liturgy of the Ordinary: Sacred Practices in Everyday Life (IVP). Her articles and essays can be found in *Christianity Today, CT Women, Art House America, Comment Magazine, The Well, Christ and Pop Culture, The Point Magazine*, and elsewhere. She is a founding member of The Pelican Project.

Greg Goebel is the founder of AnglicanPastor.com. He is an Anglican priest of the Anglican Church in North America. He served in a non-denominational church before being called into the Anglican church in 2003. He has served as an Associate Pastor, Parish Administrator, and Rector. He currently serves as the Canon to the Ordinary for the Anglican Diocese of the South.

Joshua Steele is the Managing Editor of AnglicanPastor.com. He is a priest serving at Church of the Savior in Wheaton, IL (C4SO) and a Ph.D. student in theology at Wheaton College. You can learn more at joshuapsteele.com.

Lincoln Anderson is the Lay Catechist at The Good Shepherd Anglican Church, which serves the Opelika-Auburn, Alabama, area. He is also an Aspirant to Holy Orders in the Gulf Atlantic Diocese, and blogs at WordsAndMeditation.net, which focuses on reflections of the Sunday Lectionary used by the ACNA.

Winfield Bevins is the Director of Church Planting at Asbury Theological Seminary. He is also an adjunct professor and guest lecturer at various seminaries and universities in the United States and England. Winfield has published several articles and is the author of several books, including *Ever Ancient Ever New: The Allure of Liturgy for a New Generation; Creed: Connect to the Essentials of Historic Christian Faith*; and *Our Common Prayer: A Field Guide to Common Prayer*. He is a priest in the Anglican Church in North America and serves as the Canon for Culture and Mission for the Diocese of the Carolinas.

Myles Hixson is the rector of Holy Cross Anglican Church in Knoxville, TN. He co-hosts *The Sacramentalists*, an Anglican theology podcast, and is a regular contributor to *Earth & Altar* (earthaltar.org).

Kolby Kerr serves as a bi-vocational minister at Restoration Anglican Church and high school English teacher in Richardson, Texas. He has contributed to *Anglican Pastor* and several literary and educational publications. Kolby and his wife, Emily, have two sons, Beckett and Samuel, who generally keep him busy the rest of the time.

Jack King is the rector of Apostles Anglican Church in Knoxville, Tennessee. Jack began pastoral ministry in 2004, serving in North East England before returning to Knoxville, his hometown, in 2005. Jack received a B.A. in History from Samford University and a Master of Divinity from Duke Divinity School.

Michael Matlock is an assisting priest at St. Andrew's in Versailles, Kentucky and a professor of Inductive Biblical Studies, Old Testament and Early Judaism at Asbury Theological Seminary. Fr. Michael serves as the chair of the Department of Inductive Biblical Studies and co-director of the Anglican Formation and Studies program.

Gerald R. McDermott is Anglican Chair of Divinity at Beeson Divinity School. The author or editor of 23 books, he teaches courses in Anglicanism, history and doctrine, theology of world religions, and Jonathan Edwards. His *The Future of Orthodox Anglicanism* will appear in February 2020.

Erin Faith Moniz serves as the Assistant Chaplain for Berry College. She has been in student ministry in Georgia and Tennessee for over fifteen years. She is ordained as a Vocational Deacon in the Anglican Church of North America. Erin is a trained Christian Conciliator with Peacemaker Ministries and loves getting to serve the campus community as a minister and conflict counselor. She is currently a doctoral candidate in the Doctor of Ministry program at Trinity School for Ministry researching theology of intimacy.

CONTRIBUTORS

Lee Nelson is the founding rector of Christ Church, Waco, a parish church of the Diocese of Fort Worth in the Anglican Church in North America. He also leads catechesis initiatives in the Anglican Church and was part of the team that wrote *To Be a Christian: An Anglican Catechism*. Fr. Lee believes that the time has come for the Church to revitalize the ancient practice of catechesis, grounding her members in the doctrinal, spiritual, and moral foundations of biblical and catholic orthodoxy.

Cameron Robinson is a middle school teacher, the founder of The Emmanuel Initiative, and an Air Force Reserve Chaplain. He believes that the local public school is a critical mission field and works to explore ways in which the local parish can be connected to the local school. You can read his blog at https://www.arthurcameronblog.com/ or follow him on social media: @_RevCameron.

Michael Rosengren and his wife, Nancy, are members of Ascension Anglican Church in Bakersfield, California. He is a semi-retired Marriage and Family Therapist in a part-time private practice. He is currently serving the church as a LEM and a lay reader. He is studying to become a catechist.

Peter Smith is the rector at Living Faith Anglican Church in Tempe, Arizona. As a pastor, Peter is passionate about preaching and teaching, sharing the sacraments, discipling, shepherding, and living on mission for Christ. With his free time, Peter enjoys good conversation, craft beverages, being outside, riding his scooter, playing with a ball of any kind, and spending time with his family.

Rachel Wilhelm is the United States Team Leader at United Adoration (ACNA) and Director of Worship Arts and Artist in Residence at Redeemer Anglican Church in Dacula, Georgia. She released her full-length album, "Songs of Lament," in 2017.

Whether you're an Anglican leader or just "Angli-curious," Anglican Compass has the resources you need to follow Jesus in the Anglican way. We write with clarity and charity about the Anglican tradition, in order to enrich churches on the ground today.

If you'd like to take advantage of what we have to offer, please subscribe to our email list at anglicancompass.com/subscribe.

In exchange for your email address, we will give you the latest edition of our Daily Office Booklet, an easy-to-use resource for doing Morning and Evening Prayer on your own or with a group!

Get your FREE Daily Office Booklet at anglicancompass.com/subscribe.

Made in the USA
Columbia, SC
18 February 2021

33207126R00095